Waiting for the Presence:

Spirituality of Pilgrimage to the Holy Land

*Rev. Robert Wild
of Madonna House*

WIPF & STOCK · Eugene, Oregon

Wipf and Stock Publishers
199 W 8th Ave, Suite 3
Eugene, OR 97401

Waiting for the Presence
Spirituality of Pilgrimage to the Holy Land
By Wild, Robert
Copyright©1988 by Wild, Robert
ISBN 13: 978-1-5326-3997-5
Publication date 2/22/2018
Previously published by Franciscan Printing Press, 1988

INTRODUCTION

The main purpose of this book is to foster a true spirit of Christian pilgrimage by sharing what the Lord taught me on a recent trip to the Holy Land.

From the earliest centuries Christians began to make their prayerful way to the sacred places where Jesus lived and suffered and appeared after his resurrection. They wanted to say thank you for his coming. They wanted to ask for a healing, or a special favor. Sometimes they went in reparation for their sins; or perhaps they simply sought a deepening of their faith. Whatever the reason, pilgrimage was one of the forms taken by Christian love and devotion.

There is a great deal of tourism today which goes by the name of pilgrimage. Very often, attitudes of tourism and pilgrimage are mixed. I believe the interior attitudes are really different. With this book I seek to deepen the interior attitude of pilgrimage, with the prayer that all tourists to sacred places may become pilgrims.

What is a pilgrim ? In searching for an answer to this question I asked myself, "Was Jesus ever a pilgrim ?" The Son of God has come to teach us the mysteries of the kingdom, what our hearts should be like before the Father. Was he ever a pilgrim ?

Yes. St. Luke tells us that "His parents used to go up to Jerusalem every year for the feast of the Passover" (2:41). The key to understanding Christian pilgrimage is to enter deeply into the dispositions of Jesus as he went to Jerusalem every year.

What must have been the gratitude, the praise, the devotion of Jesus as he traveled to Jerusalem to thank his Father for his great deeds of glory on Israel's behalf ! Is it too far-fetched to hear Jesus, his Mother, St. Joseph, and their relatives, singing, as they made their way along the roads from Nazareth to Jerusalem: " I rejoiced because they said to me, ' We will go up to the house of the Lord.' And now we have set foot within your gates, O Jerusalem." With what profound joy and thanksgiving Jesus must have sung and prayed that eloquent pilgrim song!

It's a long walk from Nazareth to Jerusalem. Hot too. I'm sure Jesus' thoughts turned to Israel's trek through the wilderness, and to the final crossing over the Jordan into the promised land. His fatigue and thirst and other inconveniences were offered to his Father in a spirit of penance and reparation, which is also a part of pilgrimage.

Our minds can piously imagine many things that Jesus might have done on his pilgrimage to Jerusalem, but there is one feature of his journey we know from the scriptures to be absolutely true; it may be the most important aspect of all, the one the Spirit most wanted us to know about: when Jesus went on pilgrimage to the holy places, he lingered, for days, to pray, and to be present to his Father.

There is a mentality among Eastern peoples that visitors, pilgrims, to a holy shrine remain there until the "presence" is revealed, until the blessing of God (or the saint) has come upon them. They would often camp around for days near the sacred places until the Presence manifested Itself. Thus, they "waited for the Presence."

A real pilgrimage, as an act of devotion, has its origins in the inspiration of the Holy Spirit. It is a "prayer in motion," as it were. Like prayer, it is not in the first instance something we have decided to do (although it is that), but a response to an invitation of the Spirit. The Holy

Spirit calls us on pilgrimage, and he, therefore, has a plan for us. Just as prayer is most of all a listening and a responding to God speaking to us, so a pilgrimage is most of all an attentiveness to the Spirit's inspirations along the way. I will have more to say about this in the course of the book.

Jesus was always perfectly attentive and attuned to his Father. He could only do or say what he heard the Father doing and saying. And when he got to Jerusalem, what did he hear the Father saying? The Father told him to linger at the holy places and to forget about schedules, even if it would worry his dear Mother. There are more important things sometimes. Here, in the holy city of Jerusalem, the spirit told Jesus to stay for a while, to pray, to be about his Father's business, to discuss the scriptures with the doctors of the law.

It should be the same for us. When we go on pilgrimage the Spirit says to us: "Forget about schedules! You have come to timeless, eternal places, where the mysteries of your redemption fill the air. Here there are no timetables. Listen, and wait for the Presence."

Shortly before I left on pilgrimage I asked one of the priests here at Madonna House, Father Briere, for a word for my pilgrimage. He prayed for a moment and then said: "Be present to the Holy." It proved to be a very profound word for me; it was very close to the Eastern concept I have just mentioned of "waiting for the Presence."

According to my faith, I was going to the holiest places on earth. "Take off your shoes, for the places are holy." These shrines are

I asked Fr. Briere for a word for my pilgrimage. He prayed for a moment and then said: "Be present to the Holy". It was very close to the Eastern concept of "waiting for the Presence".

saturated with the presence of Christ, with the mysteries of his life and death and resurrection. It is of the very essence of pilgrimage to, like Jesus, linger, be present, enter into the divine atmosphere of the shrines. Our Western minds have lost much of our belief in sacred atmospheres.

I was praying in the Cave of Bethlehem one afternoon and a tour came through. After giving the usual little speech on the historicity of the site, etc., the guide said: "And now, before we leave, *in order to create a little atmosphere,* let's sing one verse of 'O Little Town of Bethlehem.' " If there's any place on earth we do *not* have to create any atmosphere it is in the Cave of Bethlehem! The Presence is there; the sacred mysteries saturate the air. All we have to do is wait on the Presence, be present to the Holy.

Even before speaking and meditating about the Lord's interior attitudes on pilgrimage, we have the very significant fact that he *made one.* Of course, it is not essential to make pilgrimages; one can get to heaven without them; one can become holy without them; most of the saints never went to the Holy Land. But what I want to speak briefly about here are some attitudes which down-play pilgrimage as a source of grace and as a means of growing in faith. In our day public signs and manifestations of faith are dwindling. Pilgrimage is one of these manifestations which needs to be revitalized.

There is a letter by one of the Fathers of the Church which gives classical expression to these negative attitudes towards pilgrimage. And curiously enough, that Father is Gregory of Nyssa (4th cent.) I say "curiously enough" because this letter of Gregory "On Pilgrimages" struck me as very uncharacteristic of him. (If you've never read anything by him, please don't take this as typical). He is the great Father of describing the soul's journey, pilgrimage, to God – out of Egypt, through the desert, and into the promised land. I would think that he would have had beautiful things to say about a journey to the Holy Land, but he doesn't.

I think maybe he really didn't want to go to the Holy Land. He was sent there on some ecclesiastical business, and he had a bad experience. He lists all the reasons why people need *not* go up to Jerusalem! If you have any of these attitudes, I would like to persuade you to drop them.

The first obvious point Gregory makes is that Christ is not more present in Jerusalem than in Cappadocia (read New York), so why go there ?

> What advantage is reaped by him who reaches those celebrated spots themselves ? He cannot imagine that our Lord is living, in the body, there at the present day, but has gone away from us foreigners; or that the Holy Spirit is in abundance at Jerusalem, but unable to travel as far as Cappadocia.

Secondly, as a proof that Christ is not more present in the Holy Land than in Cappadocia, all you have to do is see the sinning that goes on in Palestine:

> Again, if divine grace was more abundant in Jerusalem than elsewhere,

sin would not be so much the fashion amongst those who live there. Well, in a place where such things go on (he lists many kinds of sins) what proof, I ask, have you of the abundance of divine grace ?

Thirdly, pilgrimaging to the holy places is no guarantee that your faith will increase:

> We confessed that Christ who was manifested is very God as much before as after our sojourn at Jerusalem; our faith in him was not increased afterwards any more than it was diminished. Before we saw Bethlehem we knew his being made man by means of the Virgin; before we saw his grave we believed in his Resurrection from the dead; apart from seeing the Mount of Olives, we confessed that his Ascension into heaven was real. Our own places are far holier than those abroad.

And then he makes the point that you don't have to go anywhere to grow in faith:

> Wherefore, O ye who fear the Lord, praise him in the places where ye are now. Change of places does not effect any drawing nearer unto God, but wherever thou mayest be, God will come to thee, if the chambers of thy soul be found of such a sort that he can dwell in thee and walk in thee.

Finally, if you go to Jerusalem with sin in your heart, it will profit you nothing:

If thou keepest thine inner man full of wicked thoughts, even if thou wast on Golgotha, even if thou stoodest on the memorial-rock of the Resurrection, thou will be as far away from receiving Christ into thyself as one who has not even begun to confess him. Therefore, my beloved friend, counsel the brethren to be absent from the body to go to our Lord, rather than be absent from Cappadocia to go to Palestine.

We share more deeply in the Spirit through our faith, "not in consequence of (a) pilgrimage to Jerusalem."

I would like to think that St. Gregory was having a bad day when he wrote that letter ! I would like to believe that elsewhere in his lost correspondence he described the more positive effects upon his life of visiting the places where Christ lived and died. It's hard for me to believe that he who loved the Lord so much could have gone there without any positive results.

I cite these negative remarks of Gregory because they are classical expressions of attitude that may be keeping some Christians from appreciating the graces of pilgrimage. I am not comparing myself with Gregory of Nyssa (!), but my experience of the Holy Land was just the opposite of his; it has also been positive for millions of other Christians down through the centuries. I recognize the obvious truth of what Gregory says, but surely it is a one-sided reflection on a pilgrimage to Palestine.

For it is also true that you can *combine*

faith with visiting the holy places. If you can come to Christ in New York, you can come to him in Nazareth. Neither should we minimize the astounding fact that Jesus never walked bodily in New York, but he did in Nazareth.

Our faith is incarnational from first to last. Christianity is not a mystical doctrine elaborated by some unknown thinker in some unknown place. Our faith is directed to God who became Man, and who was born somewhere and lived somewhere and died somewhere and rose somewhere. What Christian would not desire to see and touch such places!

The key to pilgrimage, therefore, from first to last, is faith. I didn't need to go to the Holy Land to increase my faith, but going to the Holy Land in faith increased my faith. Yes, the Cave and Tomb are empty; in one sense we don't even need them to be accessible to us. But I'm so grateful to God they are available. In some religions you *must* go to a certain holy place as part of your salvation. For us, Christ is risen and present everywhere. So, yes, we can come to him anywhere, any time, but it was wonderful to walk where he walked, and to see what he saw.

And yes, when you go to the Holy Lnad you see that the place is full of sinners, like Cappadocia and New York. I wasn't really scandalized! I didn't expect to see some miraculous land of bliss reflecting the paradise of the new creation. Especially these days! I just wanted to touch the land Jesus made holy by living on it, and I did. Faith is the deciding factor. Faith is everything.

One afternoon, again in the Cave of Bethlehem, I was praying alone. A young man, obviously an American, came in, dressed in shorts, with back-pack, camera and all. He stood in front of the Crib with a rather pained and frustrated look on his face. After about five minutes he came over to me and said, "Is this it ?" implying, "is this all there is to it ?" I said, "Yes, this is the traditional spot where Christ was born." That's all I said. I felt like saying, "The rest is your faith. The Mother and Child are not here except through faith. You should have seen it 2,000 years ago!"

He went back and continued to stand there for another five minutes. He never knelt down or made any outward sign of faith. Then he walked quietly away.

This young man became a symbol for me of those who come to the shrines without faith (not judging him, of course; I don't really know). But it's true: the tomb is empty, the manger is bare, and our poor human efforts to beautify the shrines are often very disappointing. Yet, to the eyes of faith, Christ is present in Gethsemane, weeping, glorious on Tabor, and resting in his Mother's arms in the Cave. Faith does not ask sceptically, "Is this it ?" Faith exults with a statement of fact: "This is *it !*" Faith is the key to pilgrimage.

CHAPTER ONE

PREPARATION

It's ideal if one can prepare for a pilgrimage. A few days of retreat in prayer and reflection would be beneficial. Probably most people who go on pilgrimages are on such tight schedules that they suddenly find themselves *there*, without having had a chance to wind down interiorly from their ordinary busyness. This chapter is an account of how my pilgrimage began, and how I prepared for it. I hope all prospective pilgrims will find herein some helpful suggestions.

How did my pilgrimage get started ? I was going over one of Archbishop Raya's manuscripts with him, a section on Israel. (He is a member of our community and the former Melkite Archbishop of Haifa and Galilee). He turned to me, stared intently into my eyes, and said with a delightful twinkle: "How would you like to go to the Holy Land ?" For the first half-second I thought he was kidding; then it was obvious he wasn't. I considered the question for about two seconds and then said, "Oh all right!" He offered to pay my way.

I had always wanted to go to the Holy Land but never really thought too much about it. In God's time it would happen. This, it seemed, was God's time. The Archbishop was planning to spend a year or so in Lebanon, working with the Melkite seminaries. Besides seeing the Holy Land, I would also be able to visit him in Lebanon.

Lebanon was a war-torn land at that time. It had, though, a very special attraction for me: Lebanon was the home of the patron saint of

Lebanon was the home of the patron saint of my poustinia, St. Charbel. Since I would not be able to visit his monastery and tomb, I would make him my constant companion. He would be the patron saint of my pilgrimage.

my poustinia, St. Charbel. He was a Lebanese hermit, a true molchanik, silent one. He was a member of the Lebanese Maronite Order. In 1875 he began the life of a hermit, dedicating his life to prayer, fasting and manual labor, which ended twenty-three years later with his death at the age of 70 in 1898. He was beatified by Pope Paul December 5, 1965. When Thomas Merton first heard of him he wrote:

> Charbel lived as a hermit in Lebanon -- he was a Maronite. He died. Everyone forgot about him. Fifty years later his body was discovered incorrupt and in a short time he worked over 600 miracles. He is my new companion. My road has taken a new turning. It seems to me that I have been asleep for 9 years -- and before that I was dead. *Sign of Jonas*

Actually, several months before this offer by the Archbishop, I had been thinking of pilgrimage. It's a traditional, meaningful act of piety and devotion that should be fostered and kept alive. I was on holiday in Buffalo, and I encountered a high school "March For Leukemia." I thought to myself: These marches are actually secularized versions of the Christian pilgrimage. There is the walking, the "penitence," the altruism, a destination, and people are helped. It's all there, only in a secular mode. It shows how fundamentally human the pilgrimage instinct is.

A pilgrimage is an act of devotion. It is not a holiday, not a sight-seeing tour. Usually one goes on a pilgrimage for some special faith-purpose, as I mentioned before. As I began to pray about my pilgrimage the motive of thanksgiving quickly predominated. This was the Holy Year of the Redeemer, 1983-84. Yes, it would be a pilgrimage of thanksgiving for life, for my faith, for my vocation, for my priesthood, for Redemption – for everything I have received, countless blessing upon blessing.

Because of my love for solitude, my thoughts also turned to the desert fathers and the origins of monasticism. Egypt and Sinai and Qumran and Mt. Athos came to mind. The Lord seemed to be leading me into a pilgrimage of origins, a pilgrimage to the sources of spiritual life. Yes, a pilgrimage of thanksgiving, but not simply for personal favors: thanksgiving for Jesus and the Church; thanksgiving for St. Anthony and St. Pachomius; thanksgiving for St. Athanasius of Mt. Athos.

A pilgrimage, a real pilgrimage ! Had I ever really gone on one before ? I remembered the shrines our family used to visit every summer. Before I was out of high school I had been to all the major shrines of North America -- Auriesville, St. Annè de Beaupre, St. Joseph's Oratory in Montreal, the Jesuit Martyrs at Midland, Ontario, the National Shrine of Our Lady in Washington, D.C. These were pilgrimages of sorts, but also part of our summer holidays. We certainly had the simple experiences of seeing these holy places and praying for favors, as pilgrims do. Many of these visits to shrines are indelibly impressed upon my memory and heart.

I remember my father and mother at St. Anne's going up the holy stairs on their knees. I remember the crosses on all the trees at Auriesville. I remember the statue of St. Anne surrounded with canes and crutches, and even a few

Catherine de Hueck Doherty

She removed her hand from my head, and then I said: "Catherine, do you have a word for my pilgrimage?" She remained silent for a minute or two and then said: "Explosion! God is going to explode you into himself."

It occurred to me also here in the Milk Grotto with the statue of the Flight into Egypt that Mary was a refugee, as well; and there are so many millions today.

wheel-chairs. I remember the awesomenesss of the mosaics of Christ at the National Shrine of Our Lady, and being frightened by it. I remember peering into the little room in Montreal where Brother Andre fought the devils. But these visits were mixed with holidays and vacation things.

Had I ever really gone on a pilgrimage, plain and simple? No, I hadn't. I began to get more excited. As the Lord kept drawing me into the mystery of pilgrimage, the thought kept coming to me: "Why don't you make a *real* pilgrimage – not a holiday, not a vacation, but an honest to goodness pilgrimage, with prayer and fasting and whatever else pilgrims do."

What do pilgrims do, how do they act, how do they travel?

A real pilgrim walks. Well, since I was going to the Holy Land and Mount Athos, it was obvious I couldn't walk there. In all honesty I think I would be able to walk, would like to walk. But I don't have time.

Time! Our lives are controlled by it ! Pilgrims in the early centuries used to take years out of their lives to make a pilgrimage. Why can't *we* ? Because we don't have the time. We have schedules and commitments and appointments. Maybe some day I'll be able to walk the whole way of a pilgrimage, but not now. Lord have mercy on me ! I'll be flying into the Holy Land on El Al, and entering the holiest city on earth in a crowded sherut ! My Master rode in on a donkey, and I'll be driving in in a taxi!

What do pilgrims do, how do they behave ? In preparation, I thought I'd re-read Catherine De Hueck Doherty's book *Strannik* (Pilgrim) and get some guidelines.

In a simple yet open way I wanted to proclaim to people that I was a Christian, on my way to the Holy Land to thank God for sending His Son into the world. Wearing an icon would be just perfect!

"The preparations for ... pilgrimages were very simple. You had to get a bag made out of linen. In it would be a loaf of black bread and a little salt. Then there would be an icon on a cord hanging in front."

That's what I'll do, wear an icon ! When going on holidays I usually wish to remain incognito, and avoid people as much as possible ! As I prepared for this pilgrimage I discovered a different spirit growing within me. It was a spirit of wanting to be known, a positive spirit of witnessing to Christ during this Holy Year of the Redemption. I wanted this pilgrimage to be an overt act of faith in Christ my Saviour. In a simple yet open way I wanted to proclaim to people that I was a Christian, on my way to the Holy Land to thank God for sending his Son into the World. Wearing an icon would be just perfect !

I decoupage icon prints as a hobby. I found a small, 3 x 4 Russian icon of Christ the Redeemer. I decoupaged it and put it on a black cord. I'll wear it everywhere. If people ask about it, I'll tell them I'm a pilgrim on my way to the Holy Land. If it draws a blessing, I'll praise God. If it draws anger or ridicule or scorn, I'll praise God as well – or at least I'll try. Hostility to sacred symbols is growing these days.

At table recently the topic of reactions caused by the silver cross we wear came up. Several people remarked that our cross sometimes arouses anger and resentments. One of our men was almost attacked in the wash room of a bus terminal. Father Briere told us that when he went on pilgrimage to Russia his clerical clothes caused a very violent reaction from a man in an elevator. "The pilgrim must love those who hate him and be good to those who are not good to him, even to the point of giving away his clothing and belongings." "It is part of the vocation of the Christian to bear the anger of the world" (Staretz Siloan).

When people violently react to religious symbols like that, it is not the person (in this case) wearing them who is being attacked. It is the "anger of the world" to be borne for love of that person, and in reparation for the sins of the world which have caused such anger. "Lord, give me the strength to bear any such anger that shall come my way in union with your suffering of all the anger of the world on the cross."

"The pilgrim is totally open. He is not afraid of persecution. He accepts persecution because he is the follower of a persecuted God. A pilgrim is a person of pain. If he is not ready to accept pain, he cannot be a pilgrim."

"Jesus, help me to be a real pilgrim. Help me to bear any hardships in reparation for my sins and the sins of the world. Help me to identify with you, the Supreme Pilgrim, who came and walked our earth and bore all our hatreds and scorn and misunderstandings. Lord, in some real way you still walk the earth in your members, and you will be walking again in me. I unite myself to you. Walk with me, Lord, walk with me."

"Remember that pilgrims pray all the time."

Once, when I was in Catherine's poustinia, I saw an Eastern rite cloth rosary (chotki) hanging over one of her icons. I thought of asking her if I could take that along. It will be a real aid to "praying as I go." Sight-seeing has no appeal for me right now. The only sights I'm interested in are within, and to be attentive to the graces God will have awaiting me along the way. I want to be attentive to the pilgrim plan he has for me.

Two prayers began praying themselves in my heart even before I left. The first flowed from the scripture text, "God so loved the world that he gave his only begotten Son." My prayer was simply, "Father, thank you for sending your Son." I was moved to constantly pray this prayer of thanksgiving for the coming of Christ into our world. The second prayer was inspired by the text, "He was in the world, the world was made through him, but the world did not recognize him, did not know who he was." Thus my second prayer was a form of the Jesus prayer "Lord Jesus, Son of the living God, have mercy on us for not recognizing you". I wanted to pray a prayer of mercy for the failure of humanity to recognize God when he came. Most of the human race still does not believe in him.

"The function of being a pilgrim is first and foremost poverty, that strange kind of poverty that doesn't incline too drastically or hurriedly to changes of life. The pilgrim views everything he has and is as belonging to God and his brethren."

I realized that a real pilgrim would go forth without anything but the bare necessities. I am not ready for that yet; maybe some day. What will I take along on this trip? One small piece of luggage which I can carry on the plane. I will take along only the clothes I really need. Funny, if you ask that question sincerely – "What do I *need* ?" -- you actually need very little. You need at least one change of clothes; most of the other clothes we take along are for "style." A pilgrim should not be style-conscious. You also need some warm pieces of clothing for possible change of weather. So much for clothes.

What about money ? Here I know I lack faith. I will take along some money. Yes, it's for security. Yes, it's a lack of trust in God. However, I don't have to use it like water. I want to buy some gifts from the holy places for people I love. Also, the pilgrim "gives things away." I will be attentive to opportunities of helping people along the way. No doubt the money the Lord has given me (mostly through the generosity of others) is not only for myself but for those in need I will meet. "You gave alms to the poor and you pilgrimaged to the holy places. The temptation of the pilgrim is that his hands will slowly form into fists so that he can hold onto the gifts for himself." "Lord, help me to see you as I pilgrimage along the roads. Help me to be generous as was the Good Samaritan."

When we are travelling in strange places without friendly contacts, without knowing exactly where we may be spending the night, often without knowing the language, it is very easy to be *anxious*. I know that I am being called to pray and be free from all anxiety on my pilgrimage, to really trust God for everything. I don't want to be so anxious about my own needs that I fail to see the needs of others. "Oh Lord, let me not be like the priest on the road who passed by the needy. I will be praying for mercy because the world has not recognized you. Save me from being unaware of you in my brothers and sisters as I travel to the holy places. Let me recognize the needy strangers along the way as the holiest sanctuaries of all."

Who would be my patron on my pilgrimage? As the time for my departure approached it became clear that I would not be able to visit Lebanon. The fighting was too erratic, and thus too dangerous for traveling. This was a great disappointment, but it was prudent not to go.

Since I would not be able to visit Charbel's monastery and tomb, I would make him my constant companion on my pilgrimage; he would also be my patron. One of my favorite passages in *Strannik* inspired me for this choice:

> I realize that the pilgrim is one who also stands still. It is not easy to stand still. It requires a tremendous amount of patience, and it requires a tremendous faith in God that is almost unshakable. Yes, a pilgrimage is also standing still. You will stand in perfect stillness because your hands and feet are nailed. You are unable to walk. That's a pilgrimage too. In fact, it is a supreme pilgrimage. In a way, a crown of pilgrimages.

The supreme pilgrimage is this perfect stillness before God which comes from having traversed the unimaginable distance between the soul and God. Charbel probably never traveled very far from his home town; certainly he never left his home country. He has become for me the perfect icon of the God-traveler. The unimaginable distances in interstellar space are nothing compared to the interior distances to be traveled into the heart of God. Charbel would be a perfect patron for my pilgrimage. He achieved the goal of all pilgrimages – union with God. He lived perfectly the poustinia of the heart, became the perfect pilgrim in his endless standing before the face of God in solitude.

I have a precious relic of Charbel given to me by Archbishop Raya. In 1950 Charbel's body was exhumed because of a liquid seeping from his tomb. Among other features of this investingation, the cedar bottom of his coffin was found to be rotted away. Some monks who knew Charbel were present at this exhumation in 1950.

One monk had obtained some fragments of this cedar coffin, and when Archbishop Raya visited the monastery last he obtained some of these fragments for me ! They are probably among my most prized possessions. I will take them with me as I pilgrimage, and if the Lord so wills, use them to bless people along the way.

"St. Charbel, you who never traveled beyond your borders, travel with me on my pilgrimage. Obtain for me the grace to always be on this supreme pilgrimage of perfect stillness, in the airports, in the buses, on the streets, in the restaurants, in all the journeyings which are before me."

The community was particularly excited about my going to Mount Athos. Not that it is more important than the Holy Land, but many people from our community have been to the Holy Land, but no one has ever visited Athos. Our great love for the Eastern dimension of the Church endears this holy place to us. Staretz Silouan (whom I quoted earlier) was from the

Russian Monastery of Panteleimon on Athos. He is a special favorite of ours. Also, the icon of Christ from the Serbian Monastery of Chilandari is one of our favorites; we have a print in our island chapel.

The last line I read in one of the books about Athos whetted my appetite all the more. The author (Loch) was speaking about the tourist problem, about "the tourist who was ousting the pilgrim, the sightseer who ran up and down either coast of the Mountain in a motor-boat." He concludes: "But in this motor-boat age is it possible to find numbers of men whose fullest way of self-expression in the world is to be found by withdrawing from it ?"

It *is* a vocation for some people to seek their fullest self-expression in this way; I believe it is my way. I desire to touch the places where Anthony and Pachomius founded schools of holiness which have lasted a thousand or sixteen-hundred years. "Behold, those who practice alms and completely show their love of neighbor by bodily things, are many in the world. But those who beautifully serve in solitude and have intercourse with God are scarcely to be found" (Isaac of Syria). What are the ingredients of permanence ? How does a way of life last a thousand years ? What is the beauty of the desert which is so attractive ? I had read much about Athos. Now I wanted to touch it and see it.

This pilgrimage, even before it begins, is already proving to be some kind of turning point in my life, and I think it has to do with deeper solitude. In reading about Charbel these last few days I discovered that he entered deep solitude when he was 47 years old. I just turned 47 this past October. In some ways I'm in the prime of my life. I've edited and written books, my own and others. I guess I could keep doing that. But there's some new stage I'm approaching. Deep solitude has always been the great desire of my heart. I believe I'm ready. I want to give these best years of my life to the direct seeking and service of Christ in solitude. Maybe my touching the deserts now will be the final grace and push.

"Jesus, the Supreme Solitary, enlighten me. John the Baptist, Anthony, Pachomius, Euthymius, Sabas, Theodosius, Chariton, Hilarion, John Maron, Athanasius of Athos, Nil of Sora, Seraphim of Sarov, Theophane the Recluse, pray for me. If I am to follow you here in the forest-thebaid of the New World, intercede for me."

Two days before I left, on the eve of our Foundation Day (the anniversary of Catherine's going into the poor sections of Toronto), I went over to see her, to get her blessing for my pilgrimage.

She was alone. One faint light gave a calm and peaceful atmosphere to her cabin. I bowed to the icons and greeted her as I always do: "Peace be with you." She said, "Oh, off on your pilgrimage!" I said, "Yes, and I've come to ask your blessing. In *Strannik* it says that pilgrims should get a blessing from their parents." She put her hand on my head and prayed quietly for a few moments. Then she said, "It's going to be a wonderful pilgrimage. Wonderful."

She removed her hand from my head, and then I said, "Catherine, do you have a word for me for my pilgrimage?" She remained silent for a minute or two, then said: "Explosion! God is going to explode you into himself. I will pray to

Our Lady that she obtain this explosion for you. Yes, explosion!"

I said, "That's a wonderful word. Thank you." I then told her this was going to be a pilgrimage of thanksgiving, and that I was also thanking God for her and for all she has done for me. I said I would see her in five weeks. She smiled, and I kissed her.

I started to leave the room, but then I turned abruptly and asked her if I could take with me her Eastern rite cloth rosary to pray with on my pilgrimage. She said, "Sure -- but bring it back !" I said I would and quietly slipped out the door and returned to my poustinia.

CHAPTER TWO

DEPARTURE AND ARRIVAL

The day for departure arrived. It was Sunday, October 16. I finished packing my own small suitcase and put on my pilgrim traveling clothes. I had decided to wear a tan clerical shirt and brown suit, enough to give my priesthood visibility without looking forward to wearing blacks in the heat and dust of Palestine. Before leaving the poustinia for the community Mass I prayed for a passage from Scripture. It was the scene in the Garden of Gethsemane. This word about the lonely and suffering Christ proved to be one of the two major words spoken to me on my pilgrimage. Then I went to chapel.

I wanted to give my leave-taking, and my pilgrimage in general, a communal dimension. I didn't want it to be simply "my pilgrimage" but a pilgrimage in the name of the community. So I put my little pilgrimage icon on the alter before Mass in order to have it blessed by nearness to the Sacred Gifts. The psalm for that Sunday appropriately enough was Ps. 122, "I rejoiced when I heard them say, 'Let us go to God's house.' And now our feet are standing within your courts, O Jerusalem." (Maybe the schola picked that text just for me!)

The readings also were very providential. The theme was persevering prayer. The Old Testament lesson was the story of Moses with his two arms raised in prayer during the battle with the Amalekites. This is the traditional symbol used by the Church for the contemplative life . I believed this pilgrimage would be a deepening for me of my vocation to prayer and penance within the Church.

Some of the places I was planning to visit -- monasteries in Palestine, on Mount Athos, the Carthusians -- what were they but the continuation, down through the centuries, of that prayer of Moses upon the mountain ? The Gospel was the story of the unjust judge whom the widow would not leave alone until he rendered justice. It too was a word of perseverance in prayer on my pilgrimage.

During the pause after communion I got up from my seat, took the icon off the altar, and addressed the community: "Most of you know that I leave today on my pilgrimage to the Holy Land and Mount Athos. I want you to know that I take you all with me, and that I am going in your name as well as my own. I am going to put on my pilgrim icon now, and then kneel before the icon of Christ. My pilgrimage is in honor of Christ the Redeemer, in thanksgiving for his redemption, and in reparation for our unbelief. As the priests come around and pray over me, I invite you to pray also." Then I knelt down with my own little icon around my neck for the first time. The priests prayed over me their prayers of protection and blessing, and the community joined in as well.

I think it's appropriate if, before people go on a pilgrimage, they can receive some public blessing, say, in the parish church. It would help to revive pilgrimage as a true devotion in the consciousness of our people.

Shortly after I sat down, one of the women of the community, Rejeanne, came over and kissed my icon. It was a lovely gesture which brought home to me the holiness of my adventure and the reverence with which the community was accompanying me. Before I left that day several other people kissed my icon. One had tears in her eyes. Another said, "We're all going with you." This reverencing of my pilgrim icon by members of the community was their way of consecrating my journey. I received many kinds of reactions to my little icon on my pilgrimage (which I will relate), but no one graced it with as much love as my own brothers and sisters on the day of my departure.

Another thing I did to give my pilgrimage a communal dimension was to put up an envelope marked "Intentions for Fr. Wild's Pilgrimage." Prayer for others is an important part of a pilgrimage. Our friend Gregory of Nyssa might say, "You can pray just as well in Combermere as in Jerusalem; and your prayers don't have more value in Nazareth than in Cappadocia."

But there's another instinct from God at work in us as well. There *is* something special about having a friend of yours pray for you before the Holy Crib at Bethlehem. We don't have to make a complicated theological problem out of it. To try and explain it is to be in danger of explaining it away. We know we can pray anywhere for anybody, and that God is everywhere. But we're thrilled if somebody speaks our name to God on Calvary, or at the Holy Sepulchre. Praying for someone makes that person present. I think by praying for people in the tomb of Christ, we bring them there. Through our prayer for others we bring them with us into all the sacred places.

So I decided to do that. These intentions were a sacred trust to me. I made a promise to pray through them every day, and I did. I knew them almost by heart. It was another way of bringing the community, and all the intentions in their hearts, with me. Intentions were flowing into the envelope right up until the moment I left.

That afternoon I went by car to Ottawa and stayed overnight at St. Paul's seminary. Already on that first ride I began praying the Jesus prayer on Catherine's chotki. I read a few passages from the only book, besides the New Testament, I decided to bring along with me, *The Way of the Pilgrim.* The pilgrim was in search of true prayer. What was *I* seeking ? I was seeking a deeper faith in the Incarnation. I was seeking some new burst of life. I was seeking, or rather I felt I was approaching, some new crossroads in my life's pilgrimage; Christ had some new graces for me in the land where he lived. My life was more than half over. Was I going to die like this, without ever really becoming close to God, without ever really understanding anything about what God had done for me in Christ ?

Monday morning I celebrated Mass. It was the feast of St. Ignatius of Antioch. Antioch was in modern Lebanon. "St. Ignatius, pray for the peace of your homeland and countrymen. And help me to witness to Christ on this pilgrimage as you witnessed to him on your way to martyrdom in Rome. Oh, obtain for me from our great God and Saviour something of the courage which made you write, 'Let it be known that I will gladly die for God if only you do not stand in my way. I plead with you: show me no untimely kindness. Let me be food for the wild beasts, for they are my way to God. I am God's wheat and shall be ground by their teeth so that I may become Christ's pure bread.' "

Walking around Ottawa that day I received

the first of many stares and glances at my little icon. I must admit that I always had some apprehension in wearing it. Doubts came into my mind about offending the Jewish people by wearing it. "But why should they be offended ? Christ is their very own. They should be proud of him." Thus did I encourage myself.

I took an afternoon bus to Mirabel airport outside of Montreal. I kept saying the Jesus prayer and "Lord have mercy on us for our lack of faith in you." Going through the countryside of Quebec we passed a rather large roadside crucifix. Nobody batted an eye. The conversations continue. A crucified Man on the side of the road. What do people think when they see such an image ?

The pilgrim is up to 12,000 Lord-have-mercy's a day. I read a passage from my pocket New Testament where it says that Christ was angry, but also "he felt sorry for them because they were so stubborn and wrong." It seemed an apt description of the human race in the light of the Incarnation -- stubborn and wrong. "The human race has nothing to boast about to God."

I received a good word from the Lord about my icon which rests uncomfortably upon my faithless breast. "Everyone in the world is your brother and sister, just like the people who kissed your icon before you left. Instead of worrying how *they* will see *you,* you have the eyes of faith to see *them* properly. If everyone was freed from their ignorance and blindness, they would all kiss your icon. With the eyes of faith, see them kissing your icon in their deepest heart. And pray for them that someday they actually will."

I was subjected to rather intense – courteous

but intense -- interrogation by no less than three different Israeli immigration officials. I was asked the same questions by three officials, each one "higher up" than the previous one. Maybe my pilgrim garb seemed too artificial to be real. And then I only had one piece of luggage for five weeks abroad ! Maybe clerical clothes are one of the more common disguises used these days. I didn't blame them, really. Planes are being hijacked, and they do deal with terrorists all the time. This was my first personal contact with Israelis. Already I felt some of the tension and stress they live under. No, I didn't blame them.

After passing through the security check and walking into the waiting room, I found myself already in Israel: Everybody seemed to be Jewish but me! My first impression was, "These are all Jesus' relatives." Exodus came to mind, and all the migrations of the Jewish people down through the ages; many of them enforced by "Christians." But it was a joyful migration this evening. People were excited and happy to be travelling to Israel. But the exodus image was there.

It was an El Al night flight, non-stop, Montreal to Tel Aviv. There were hundreds of people on board, and it would take 9½ hours. I sat next to a very friendly Jewish man with whom I toasted "To Life!" with our dinner wine. We chatted off and on, nothing too serious. The plane was crowded, and most people seemed to know each other, or were making friends quickly. I dozed a little but was too excited to sleep. The crowded space gave me a sense of the mass of humanity into which Jesus had come.

My friend next to me knew I was a priest, and that I was going to visit the holy places. As he woke from one of his dozing periods he said (and he must have been pondering this for quite a while): "Judaism and Christianity are not really different. We both worship the same God."

I tried to judge if it was an important question for him, or if he was just making conversation. It seemed important, so I said: "But what about Christ ? We believe he is the Messiah. Isn't that the great difference?" "But he can't be the Messiah,"" he said, "because when the Messiah comes everything will be wonderful." "But," I said, "isn't that kind of a magical view of the Messiah ? We believe everything *would be* wonderful if people did what the Messiah said they should do. Surely the world isn't just going to become wonderful without our participation." He didn't say anything in response, and I didn't pursue it any further.

I remarked at one point about the skull caps worn by many. "That's a sign of reverence for God," he said. "Your Pope has one."

I mustered up the courage to ask him if my icon would be offensive to Jewish people in Israel. He said a very definite "I don't think so," which cheered me up.

The captain announced that we were now flying over the entire length of Yugoslavia. "Oh," I thought to myself, "maybe Our Lady is appearing to the children this very moment."

For the past several years, since June 24, 1981, Our Lady has been appearing daily to some children in the town of Medjugorje. The apparitions have not been officially approved by the Church, but neither have they been discountenanced in any way. From the testimony of many people who have been there, including priests from America and Canada, they sound very authentic. She is calling for prayer and penance for the world. I asked her to bless my pilgrimage and to accompany me along the way. I had toyed with the idea of trying to go to Medjugorje, but decided not to.

People began to get more excited. An hour and a half to Jerusalem. The noise-level rose. There was lots of noise as Christ approached Jerusalem also. Thousands of galaxies in the universe, and our God decides to touch down in ours. "And the Almighty Word leapt down...." I will be dropping down from 35,000 feet. The Word came from .... how far away ?

Landing, customs and taxi to the Via Dolorosa. As soon as we drove through the Lion's Gate I knew we must be on the Via Dolorosa, so I told the driver to stop. How can I drive in a taxi onto the Via Dolorosa ! I couldn't put those two together in my heart. From the directions I had received I knew I was not too far from Ecce Homo, where I was staying. I could walk the rest of the way.

The driver over-charged me. I knew it, but I gave him even more, to his great consternation. "If anyone takes your cloak, give him your tunic as well." I was flooded with the sense of the holiness of the place, so was in no mood to haggle. Being on the Via Dolorosa for the first time in my life, I was neither going to drive on it in a taxi, nor get upset over money!

It was night; I was tired. But I was on the Via Dolorosa. It was still awesome -- tiredness, luggage, and all. Asking a few directions I arrived at Ecce Homo which is run by the Sisters of Sion, and breathed a sigh of relief as they recognized me and led me to a room.

Before I went to supper I walked out onto the roof and for the first time in my life saw a panoramic night view of Old Jerusalem, the holiest city on earth. The symbolism of it all was too profound, too overwhelming. I just stood there in the warm, quiet night, and let thousands of years of history impact on my soul. Then I went to supper and retired early. I hadn't really slept for almost thirty-six hours.

One of the temptations of pilgrims who are alone and far away from home is to immediately start "making contacts" with people. This was never a real temptation for me, but it's a pattern that one can easily fall into if one is not vigilant.

At the places where you stay, you begin meeting people at meals and in the normal comings and goings. This can't be avoided. But out of their need, people begin asking you to go here and there with them. Often they too are alone in a far-away place and are seeking companionship.

I think pilgrims need to be kind but firm here. You have come to pray, and to follow the Holy Spirit. You can't do this very well if you're tied to traveling around and talking with other people. A guest asked me the very next morning if I wanted to go to such and such a place with him. I said no thank you. He said, "what are you going to do your first day in Jerusalem ?" I said, "Well, I don't know what other people do, but

I'm going to pray."

There *was* a temptation that first morning to rush out the front door and begin dashing around Jerusalem. After all, I had never been in this Holy Land before, so hurry up and get to it ! I had to restrain myself, or rather the Holy Spirit came to my rescue. Why was I rushing out ? I already *was* in a holy place, Ecce Homo. Slow down ! Be present to the Holy !

I went to the small chapel which overlooks the large church below. I celebrated, alone, a silent, long, prayerful liturgy. It was the feast of Isaac Jogues and the North American martyrs.
Here, for the first of many times in the Holy Land, I raised the Blood of Christ over the city and the country. On the pavement below this Blood had been spilt for love of me. The Holy Spirit clearly instructed me that morning that my daily celebration of the liturgy was the most important act I could perform as a pilgrim, and to be faithful to it. He had brought me here to pray for the peace of Jerusalem, not to sight-see, not to "make contacts," but to pray.

As I reflected that morning on the Blood of Christ spilled on the pavement below I remembered something that occured once during a liturgy. I was holding the chalice for people to drink out of, and on this particular occasion it was rather full. A woman took it, not realizing how full it was, and drank too quickly. The Precious Blood splashed over her clothes and shoes and down onto the floor.

I really was not upset; accidents happen; Jesus is not upset. But it did become a dramatic image for me of what, through our sins, we have actually done with the blood of Christ –

splattered it all over the earth. Now I was close to the spot (still hadn't gone down yet) where this spilling of his Blood was not an accident but a barbaric, willful act of creatures towards the most loving Person who ever walked our earth.

Then, after Mass, I went down to the Lithostrotos, the actual pavement where Jesus had been brought out from prison and mocked by the soldiers.

The question of whether this or that place was the "actual," "exact" site of Christ's passion, birth, etc., never bothered me. As I descended to the Lithostrotos some maps and archeological evidence appeared on the walls. I didn't stop to look. It didn't matter to me. Let the archeologists worry about it. It's a real temptation for the pilgrim to allow the problem of "Is this the exact spot?" to disturb your mind.

I believe in the Incarnation. I believe this is the Holy Land and this is the Jerusalem where he suffered. The sacred drama happened here somewhere. The whole land is holy. I would kiss every inch of it; I would gladly kiss every stone of every pavement uncovered.

The same with his birth and the other events of his life. He really was born in Bethlehem, so there's a holy cave there somewhere. The whole Sea of Galilee is holy because he walked on it and calmed it. It's whole shoreline is holy because he got in and out of boats somewhere. Every mountain in Palestine is transfigured because he was transfigured on one of them somewhere. Every hill is blessed because on one of them, somewhere, he said, "Blessed are the poor..." The actual place doesn't matter. The actual place for me is wherever I meet Christ in faith.

The archeological evidence about the holy places is interesting. I read some of it, but not much. And never did I prepare for a holy place by reading the brochures. Maybe afterwards I read some. But I had come to pray, not study, not acquire information.

Thus, when I descended to the lowest level of Ecce Homo, where the stones from the Roman courtyard of the time of Our Lord have been excavated, the first thing I did (and I did this at all the holy places on my arrival) was prostrate on the ground. What else is appropriate when you arrive for the first time in your life at the place where Christ was mocked as a Fool for love of you ! I kissed the pavement many times. I knelt and prayed. I sat for several hours, meditating and praying and being present to the Holy.

For the first time in my life this mockery and debasement of Jesus as part of a cruel game seemed the most absurd of all his sufferings for us. The flogging was an ordinary punishment; even the crucifixion was a normal form of execution. But being made a fool as part of a game !

The soldiers had a game called "The Game of the King." They were given a prisoner to make sport of. Dice and chance were involved. At the end of the game the poor victim was killed. Jesus allowed himself to be used in one of our senseless, mindless games. What abasement by the King of the Universe !

One of the graces I received at the Lithostrotos was greater courage to live the Gospel no matter how foolish people thought I was. How often I have avoided the following of Jesus

One of the graces I received at the Lithostrotos was greater courage to live the Gospel no matter how foolish people thought I was.

because it involved being considered foolish and ridiculous in the eyes of others. "Lord, cover me with your mantle of foolishness. May I never refuse to follow you because of human respect."

While praying at this sacred place of Ecce Homo I witnessed for the first time what would become a common scene during my visits to the shrines: a tour ! I may as well get off my chest here all the thoughts I had about these tours. So here goes.

Usually a tour would consist of twenty or thirty people, sometimes more, sometimes less. A guide would be with them. The people file in, then the guide gives a short speech on the history of the site, etc. The people may look around for a few moments, then they leave.

I don't know if any of these people ever come back to the sacred places after this tour. Perhaps they do. I hope so. But I suspect in many cases they do not, since they are often traveling quite a distance by bus to get to the shrines. I'm sure that for many people the first time they set foot in a sacred place is on one of these tours. I thanked God every day I was not on one !

I just could not imagine myself coming, for the first time in my life, into the courtyard where Christ was mocked, listening to a speech by a guide, and then having to file out again in a few minutes. How could anyone do that ! Here you are, in the holiest places on earth, and you file in and out in fifteen minutes!

This was, for me, a great sadness, even to witness it; as I said, I couldn't imagine being involved in it. Aren't these people aching to pray

43

and adore ? Doesn't their whole being desire to remain and meditate on these sublime mysteries of our faith ? How is it possible to breeze through these places so hurriedly ?

I realize that not everybody can go alone on a pilgrimage as I did (although I think many more people could do it if they were willing to trust God and put up with all the inconveniences.) Or they might go in twos and threes. Perhaps many people cannot even do that. What then?

Somehow the spirit of pilgrimage has been sold out to the guides and the tourist agencies. Do these people on tours *want* more time to pray and linger ? If so, why don't they inform the guides of their intentions ? The people pay the money. Why can't they pray for an hour in each of the holy places ? In an attempt to "get everything in" hundreds of thousands of people are rushed through the shrines like crowds going through turnstiles at a football stadium. I know many are praying in their hearts, and probably want to stay and pray longer. But ten minutes is all the tour guide allows. They have come half-way around the world to visit these places, and ten minutes is all they get ! It was always very sad to see, very sad indeed.

People who arrange the tours should make it clear to the agencies what it is they want. Surely they should want quality on a pilgrimage, not quantity. See less places and pray more. Don't rush through these sacred places as if you're touring a museum. Prayer and time for reflection is everything on a pilgrimage. I spent hours in many of the holy places, and saw half a dozen tours come through in the space of a couple hours. "When do they pray ?" I thought to myself.

In the Holy Land there is a difference between tourists, who come to water-ski in Eilat...

... *and pilgrims who carry the cross of Christ on the Via Dolorosa.*

Oh, I'm sure it's some kind of blessing for them. They go back home with a rich store of memories and experiences. But they will never again have the opportunity to pray *on* Calvary, or *at* the Holy Sepulchre, or *on* the Mount of Olives. This is the uniqueness of a pilgrimage: To be able to linger at the holy places like Jesus did when he went up to Jerusalem, and to wait on the Presence there.

If this book could change one "tour" to the Holy Land into a pilgrimage, it would be worthwhile! If I could convince one tour guide, one agency, to allow more time for prayer instead of dashing off to "see" the next shrine it would have been worthwhile.

One of the people I met in the Holy Land was an Arab who worked for the Jewish tourist agency. I was expressing some of these concerns to him and he simply said: "tours are not for praying, they're for making money." Have Christians sold out the spirit of pilgrimage to the spirit of tourism? I think we have. The pilgrims pay the money; they should be able to control the tour. If not, get somebody else to do what *you* want, not what the agency wants. All you have to do is threaten them that you'll go to another agency!

Another advantage of going alone and lingering at the shrines is that, if you stay long enough, you can hear what several tour guides say! I heard at least one explanation at each place just by being there over a period of time.

If you can, go yourself, or with one or two others. The places are easy to find; everybody knows where they are. Why do we need a guide to lead us to places everybody knows about!

And you can read the information in the guide books yourself if you're interested. That's where the guides read it. Be courageous. Trust God. Move at your own pace. Linger and pray. Enough! It's off my chest! I promise not to mention it again!

CHAPTER THREE
Jerusalem: Via Dolorosa, Mount of Olives

It was mid-afternoon when I decided that I had lingered long enough on the Lithostrotos (can one ever stay too long?). For the first time in daylight I stepped out the front door on to the holiest street on earth--the Via Dolorosa.

The holiest and one of the busiest! Shops galore, whose merchants and wares cry out to you like sirens. I was determined to get to the holy places first, and not be distracted by the shops. I wasn't always successful, as I will relate shortly.

First I went to the Church of the Flagellation, and my thoughts turned to all the sins of the flesh down through the centuries. "Sins of the flesh" are not only sexual, but all the ways we abuse our bodies through addictions and over-indulgences. St. Paul says we should use our bodily members to serve Christ as once we used them to serve sin. Our bodies are temples of the Holy Spirit, holy because God dwells in us. Instead of being "living sacrifices" to the glory of God, we have often made them into occasions which make Christ weep. Here he infused his love into our bodies, and won for us the power not to mock or torture them with our lust and perversions.

I recalled my own sins in these areas and looked for a priest for confession. I couldn't find one who spoke English. This was a new experience for me -- looking for a priest for confession and not being able to find one. I prayed for all those trapped in their sins of the flesh who don't know how to be released from them. I would return here again and perhaps find a priest then.

Not far from there is the pool of Bethsaida where Jesus healed the blind man. There is a lovely little park where you can sit and meditate on Jesus walking around the pools on that day when he brought the light of day and grace to that man. One of the gracious aspects of this miracle is that Jesus himself initiates the conversation: "Do you want to be healed ?". I think many times a day grace approaches us like that -- in people, in circumstances -- putting that question to us. But we are too blind or deaf to hear.

I headed back to Ecce Homo to continue along the Via Dolorosa. The shrine of "Christ In Prison" was closed. I continued on but then – temptation ! Icons in one of the shops caught my eye. I love icons. And here I am in the Holy Land, and with money, and, well, the temptation was too great. (Besides, hadn't I been praying enough all morning and most of the afternoon ! I deserved a break!) I succumbed. I entered the shop.

The owner (so he turned out to be) saw me looking at icons, and his trained eye saw I was wearing one. So, putting two and two together, he immediately said: "Come into the back of the shop and I will show you some *real* icons."

My defenses went up. I'm rather naive when it comes to buying anyhow. I know something about icons, but not much. I knew that there were many imitation icons in these shops. I knew that these guys are out to make money. I knew that they don't always tell the exact truth. Pilgrim Wild, be careful !

He showed me some icons which he said were very old. They surely looked old. Two of them in particular made my heart jump. One was of the Transfiguration, and the other was an unusual icon of the Resurrection which I had never seen before. The common Resurrection icon is of Christ descending into Hades, taking Adam and Eve by the hand, and leading them out. This icon was of the resurrected Christ in the garden. Mary Magdalen was clutching his feet, while two other women were in the background. It was exquisite ! I thought to myself that even if it was fake, I'd like to have it.

I asked him how much it was, but the price he quoted was way out of my reach. (I said as much. He looked at me and asked if I was a priest. (I was often called "Father." I guess my icon and beard told the story.) We chatted a bit. I began to tell him a little of my life, that I spent a great deal of time in prayer and solitude. I could see that something was happening in his heart.

He then began telling me a little bit about himself. He said he was a Christian, and began to witness to me about Christ. (He was an Arab. To this day I don't know if he really is a Christian or not.) He said many people come in here who trade in icons -- buying from him in order to sell to others. He doesn't like that, but there's not much he can do about it.

Then he said something which I thought was quite extraordinary even as a sales pitch. He said if I promised not to sell this icon, and to pray for him and his family every day, he would sell me this icon for less than what he paid for it himself. He then quoted me a price I was willing to pay.

Well, my defenses really went up then. Does he give this line to everybody ? Am I being taken in – and on my very first day !

Then he said: "To show you my sincerity, I'm going to let you take this icon with you without paying for it. You can check on it or me until you decide to take it or not." I walked out of the shop with this lovely icon in my hands. I thought to myself: "This icon is either genuine, or this guy is one of the greatest con artists I've ever met." (I will continue this drama later.)

I continued on my way along the Via Dolorosa, but now with this resurrection icon. (We always walk our way of the cross in the strength of the resurrection.) I came to the Station "Veronica Wipes the Face of Jesus." In Greek, *veron-ica* means "true image, true icon." It is the name tradition gave to this compassionate woman. She had the courage to wipe the Face of Christ. In gratitude he imprinted his Face , first on her being, and then on the towel, as a sign of the restoration of her deepest self to God's image and likeness.

I knelt on the pavement outside as the buying and selling, the comings and goings, swirled about me. I prayed for the grace not to allow human respect to prevent me from wiping the face of Christ in others. W.H. Auden has a poem about finding a drunk on the street. People are walking by and nobody is helping him.

Then I took him all puking, into my arms.
And staggered, banged with terror.
Through a million, billion, trillion stars.

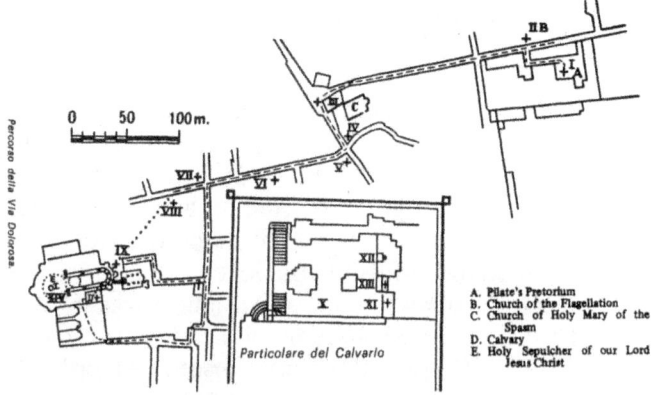

I continued on my way along the Via Dolorosa, but now with my Resurrection icon. (We always walk our way of the cross in the strength of the Resurrection).

The door to the Station was locked, so I obtained the key from one of the Little Sisters of Jesus who take care of the shrine. She knew our Madonna House team which had been stationed in Haifa a few years ago. I went upstairs and opened the door of the chapel. I suddenly found myself in a beautiful Byzantine church.

Over and over again during my trip I was to have this same experience – suddenly finding myself surrounded with great beauty. The exteriors of buildings were often drab and even dirty. But when you passed through the door you often found yourself in a lovely garden, or in an exquisite church such as the one I was now in. This experience became a symbol for me of what is often the drab exterior of a person's face or features, and the extraordinary beauty of the heart and interior life. I prayed here for half an hour before a picture of Veronica's Veil. May we all be quickly restored to the true image and likeness of Christ.

It is easy to miss some of the Stations of the Cross, especially if it's your first time, and you don't know where you're going. And there are so many shops, and the hustle and bustle of so much human activity. You're not exactly in a church.

As I continued walking I came across a sign that read, "Ethiopian Patriarchate and Monastery." "Oh," I thought, "that sounds interesting." I walked up the stairs and entered the open door.

There was a small monastery garden surrounded by a church and dwellings. I ventured farther in. I came across a monk who was very shabbily dressed praying out of his prayer book.

We both smiled in a peaceful and calm exchange. He then said a few words (I presume) in English. We both smiled.

Then he did something quite beautiful. He saw I was carrying my prayer beads. He took them from me and began to pray with them. I then took his prayer beads and began praying them as well. When he finished he simply handed mine back to me and I did the same with his. It was a real inspiration of his to meet this way, separated as we were by language and doctrine. In Christ we were not separated; prayer together to the Father united us. We both bowed to each other with another smile, and separated. These are the kinds of little grace-filled episodes that happen when you are prayerfully walking around and trying to be attentive to the Presence.

In another part of the garden a group of monks was sitting around and talking. I approached and asked if I could see the church. One monk rose and kindly took me into the first Ethiopian Church I'd ever seen. I knew something of the harsh persecutions the Christians are experiencing presently in Ethiopia. I felt I was in the presence of martyrs. The paintings and iconography struck me at once as a blending of Greek and more far-eastern styles; there was even some obvious western influence. The monk let me out through the back door of the church, different from where I had entered. All of a sudden I found myself right at the entrance to the door of the Church of the Holy Sepulchre.

My first reaction was, "I'm not ready yet!" This experience also was often to be repeated on my pilgrimage.

Not being on a guided tour, and often not knowing where I was going, I would suddenly just find myself at one of the holiest places on earth without being mentally prepared. A surprise of the Spirit you will say. It certainly was! But whenever it happened, I heard myself saying inside, "God, I'm not ready yet, I'm not ready yet. I have to get ready." God didn't listen. I was there – here – and I had to enter into the grace of the moment. The Presence was ready for me whether or not I was ready for him.

I stood for a minute or so outside the Church of the Holy Sepulchre trying to decide if I should go in. I didn't have to go in today; I could come back later, or tomorrow. I decided to enter.

If you walk straight ahead in this Church you quickly come upon a marble slab on the floor with many vigil lights hanging over it. I thought this was the Holy Sepulchre. I knelt down and kissed it and reverenced it. The holiest spot in the universe.

I was only there a few moments when I noticed that most people were walking right past this spot and on into the interior of the Church. "Is this the right place?" I thought to myself. I got up and followed a small group of people, arriving with them at last at the real tomb of Christ. (The place I had been reverencing was the commemoration of the taking down of the Lord's Body from the Cross).

Pilgrims should not be upset with such mistakes. Pilgrimaging differs from planned, moment by moment, carefully mapped out tours. The pilgrim is also on an adventure. You don't always know exactly where the holy places are. If you can be at peace about these wrong turns and mistakes, you'll be a better pilgrim. (On another occasion I went up the wrong staircase on my knees, thinking it was the stairs to Mount Calvary. Does it really matter? One still meets the Presence and receives a blessing.)

So I *finally* arrived at the real tomb of Christ, all the more magnificent now since I knew for sure that it *was* the tomb of Christ. I prostrated before it; knelt for a while; then just sat down and prayed and meditated. I clasped my Resurrection icon closer to my heart and felt something of the joy of the women on Easter. Many tours were going in and out (it was mid-afternoon), so I decided I would not enter today but come back tomorrow.

As I was sitting there a flashbulb went off inside the semi-darkness of the tomb. I thought of what a scientist had said in a film on the Holy Shroud of Turin. He said that "the only thing we (scientists) know could produce such an image on the Shroud would be something akin to a nuclear explosion." What a marvelous thought that was! At the moment of the Resurrection the Father touched the Body of Christ, and something like a nuclear explosion happened – the Resurrection! The bright flash in the tomb that afternoon became the image of that moment when, through God's almighty power, the Lord Jesus exploded back into the totality of his incarnational reality. I sat there for quite a while, clinging to my (his!) resurrection icon, and then I walked back to Ecce Homo.

That night before I went to bed, I sat and looked and looked some more at this(fake? real?)

So I finally arrived at the real tomb of Christ, all the more magnificent now since I knew for sure that it was the tomb of Christ.

icon. How I wished it was real ! With my uncritical eye I kept examining it over and over again. It looked real to me; and, if it was, it certainly was worth every penny he was asking. I'm sure, if it were real, it would be worth four times the amount in North America. What to do, what to do ?

I decided to trust him. I wouldn't ask anybody about him. I wouldn't seek any appraisal of the icon. Maybe it was foolish. I don't know. But I'm going to take it.

Next morning I went back to the shop. I told the owner that I didn't check up on him or his icon. He was visibly moved by this trust. I told him I would pray for him and his family every day, and that the icon would never be sold. Besides the price of the icon, I also gave him a sizable donation for a children's orphanage he was running. Well, if he had been conning me, this last gesture would have him come clean for sure.

Nothing changed. He stuck to his story, and I gave him the money and took my precious icon. We embraced and parted. I subsequently found out that my icon *is* real, and worth much more than what I paid for it. Grace had been present in our transaction. May God keep me faithful to my daily prayers for him !

I may as well complete here this story of the icon.

When I returned to Madonna House I told them this whole episode. I said, further, that there is some mystery behind this icon; I don't know exactly why I bought it; I felt God had some special purpose in practically giving me this icon. I asked God about it in prayer. What came to me was this.

This is an icon of hope. It should be a travelling icon. It should be where people need hope. "So," I told the community, "if you are ever depressed, if you are sick, if you are despairing, if you need an increase of joy and hope and lightness of heart, ask me for this icon. You will be able to borrow it for a while so that through its presence the gift of hope may be increased in your heart."

And that is how this icon is now used. People have taken it to the hospital during times of operations. Frequently it is in their room when they are sick. One person was having nightmares so he slept with it under his pillow ! God is good !

I returned to the Holy Sepulchre that morning with the intention of entering. I bowed to the ground at the entrance. Then I went in. There are two sections to the Holy Sepulchre, an antechamber and the inner tomb proper. I entered the antechamber of the tomb of Christ for the first time. I knelt down for ten minutes or so, preparing myself for the tomb.

Just then a monk came in dragging a prie-dieu behind him. He was making arrangements for a few elderly women to kneel before the tomb. He motioned me back just as I was about to enter. Somehow it disturbed my inner spirit. I decided these were not the circumstances under which I wanted to enter the holiest place on earth. I would wait for a quieter time. I went back outside.

It was a joy just to sit outside the tomb in these early morning hours and allow the Spirit to speak to me. The women in my icon were here those many centuries ago, sitting on the grass for hours in front of the sealed tomb. Their Master was dead. "What will happen now ? He raised other people to life. Is he that great ? Greater than death ? Can he raise himself ? Will the God he prayed to raise him ? Who *was* this Man ?"

As I was meditating such sublime thoughts a woman tourist came by and said quite loudly to her husband, pointing to the tomb, "What's that, George ? " I don't know why this remark disturbed me so much; I didn't know where the tomb was either. I guess it disturbed me because I heard in that remark my own superficiality, my own flippancy, my own incomprehension of what God has done for us.

We believe the most astounding things: God become a Man; God died for us; God has risen from the dead; God has given us himself as food. It was just that we human beings are so blind and faithless – "O you of little faith. How is it that you still do not understand? How much longer must I put up with you?" We're just so *blasé* about the most awesome truths of human existence. "What's this Cross ? What's this Blood on the ground ? What's this tomb ?" God has done too much for us. We can't get our puny minds around it. That woman was me and every other Christian, tripping and bungling around sacred tombs and crosses in a state of total incomprehension. What's this, George, indeed !?

Because of the fighting in Lebanon I was not able to visit Charbel's monastery where he lived. So he brought a monastery to me.

Later that afternoon I was walking near the

Damascus Gate when I spied a sign which read, "Maronite Monastery." I thought to myself, "Surely they will know all about Charbel." I was not disappointed. In their gift shop were many medals and pictures of Charbel. I bought some. Another gift was the priest, Father Hassad. He was a monk and had spent some time at Charbel's monastery. It was a gift from God just to meet someone that close to Charbel.

Father Hassad spent an hour with me, then gave me a tour of the monastery. (This tour I didn't mind !) In the chapel were two large pictures of Charbel. I stayed for lunch, and then came back the next day for the liturgy. I have a copy of the rite in French. It begins beautifully,

> From your light, Lord Jesus, we draw
>   our own luminosity;
> O Source of light, true light, Sun of
>   the universe,
> Make us worthy to approach your
>   dazzling light,
> And to penetrate into the splendor
>   of your joyful dawn.

The liturgy was very simple and dignified. Father Hassad said it was very ancient, antedating the liturgies of Basil and Chrysostom; it was basically the liturgy that Charbel would have celebrated in his hermitage every day. This latter fact was the most inspiring of all for me. I felt I met Charbel at this liturgy, surrounded by members of his Maronite family, and celebrating in the language and rite he used.

I learned too that the Maronites had suffered much for their faith down through the centuries. I resolved to learn more about their history.

Later that same day I was walking near the Lion's Gate, loaded down with packages. Suddenly I could not find Catherine's chotki ! I checked all my pockets many times. No chotki. I went back twice over the route I had walked. No chotki. I never did find it. It was a great loss, particularly because it brought Catherine and her intentions close to me. But, pilgrims must be detached.

When I returned home and told her that I had lost her rosary, she just shrugged, reached over to her bedside table, and handed me her personal Roman Catholic rosary to keep. That's how she is. I have often seen her praying this rosary. It will be a treasure for me to remember her by. I wouldn't have it had I not lost the first one.

I stopped at a food stand and bought some bread to eat along the way. The man said to me, in broken English, "Jesus Book. Jesus Book. I like. I like." He meant the New Testament, of course. I told him that I only had one small copy with me, and that it was not for sale. (He probably, of course, didn't understand a word I was saying. But this explanation soothed my conscience.) As I started walking away I remembered that the pilgrim in *The Way* had given away his "Jesus Book" because that very book had told him to sell all he possessed.

So, I turned around, walked back, and simply handed the guy my pocket New Testament. I could easily obtain another one, if not here, certainly when I got home. But I didn't know if my friend here would ever come across one in the near future. Maybe it will bring him to Christ. I hope so. Then I walked on towards the Mount of Olives.

One of the first places I visited on the Mount of Olives was the tomb of Mary. As was my custom, I just sat there for an hour or so, listening to the Spirit, waiting on the Presence, making a faith contact with the mysteries of grace saturating the atmosphere.

A grace I received there (and which was intensified at the Dormition Abbey) was a lessening of the fear of death, a lessening due to the realization that I would not be dying alone. Mary is the Patroness of a happy death. The icon of the Dormition ("falling asleep") pictures Mary dying with all the apostles around her.

Often, in the lives of the saints, we read how their patrons, or their loved ones, or the angels, came and were present to them at the moment of death. Thomas More's daughter, Margaret Roper, was visited, at the moment of her death, by some of the Carthusians she had ministered to in prison at great personal danger. They said to her "We have come to accompany you home."

If such heavenly escorts are true of the saints, what must have been the assembly and entourage of holy ones present to take Mary home ? Christ was there, and St. Joseph; myriads of angels; perhaps Elizabeth and Zachary, Joachim and Anne; some of her relatives and friends we know of from the Gospel. Our departure may not be so glorious, but we can be assured we will not make that immense journey alone.

Not far from this church is Gethsemane. I will not keep repeating myself, but entering each holy place for the first time was always the same: /AWESOME. I could hardly think of anything. You can't believe you're there, in these places you've been meditating on all your life. You see the centuries-old olive trees which date back to the time of Christ. You see, in the church, the huge rock where tradition says Jesus sweat his Blood. I prostrated upon it, and prayed. My heart is still too hard to weep, but I desired to weep. May the Lord take the desire for the deed.

Pilgrims without schedules get in on many surprising treats. A solemn high, Latin liturgy was just beginning, so I asked and obtained permission to concelebrate. Not only that, but when it came time for the minor elevation I was handed the chalice filled with the Precious Blood. I raised this chalice solemnly over the very rock where this Blood had been shed in dread of the coming ordeal, shed for me. It was during that Mass that I conceived the desire to spend the night in this church, watching with Christ, in reparation for all who have fallen asleep in prayer and failed to console him, including me. But this was not granted me.

Then the thought came to me: "If you're really serious about it, you can stay up all night back at Ecce Homo." While I used to get up every night for a vigil, I rarely spent the whole night in prayer. I never did do it! This was another proof to me of the often grandiose and unrealistic aspects of some of our desires in the spiritual life. I make-believe that my "great desires" (in this case an all-night vigil) are being thwarted. Nothing was keeping me from making an all-night vigil every night if I really wanted to. What illusions we have in our spiritual lives.

(This is an aside, but apropos of the above. Once one of the guests here was going on and on about how drab and ordinary life is at Madonna

House. "We should all be out on the street corners singing and shouting to all the people about the love of God," she said eloquently. When she had finished I simply said to her, "Well, why don't you ?" "Why don't I what ?" she said. "Why don't you do that ? There's nothing preventing you." She didn't say anything, and I'm sure she never did it.)

It had been already a long day so I returned to Ecce Homo for a nap. I was very happy to have discovered the Mount of Olives. I decided to return there in the early evening and watch the sun go down over Jerusalem.

As I was making my way that evening back to the Mount of Olives I passed two teenagers along the Via Dolorosa. One of them, seeing my icon, pointed to the pavement and said, "For you!" I looked down and saw some mule dung. (My prejudiced vision at the moment.) I thought that's what he was referring to, and was making a sarcastic remark. But as he passed by he said, "And for me." He meant the Passion of Christ.

As I would do several times during my stay in Jerusalem, I climbed the Mount of Olives in the early evening and just walked around, or prayed, or sat on a rock over-looking the city of Jerusalem. Christ must have come up here hundreds of times, and spent hundreds of hours in prayer. Because I believe my own vocation is praying for the world, this Mount became my favorite spot. Here is where Jesus prayed for the world and for the peace of Jerusalem. Here is where he pleaded with his Father that the world would recognize him. Here is where he taught us how to go apart and pray to the Father in secret. His disciples knew that it was in prayer to his Father that he gained his strength for the crowds

As I would do several times during my stay in Jerusalem, I climbed the Mt. of Olives in the early evening and just walked around, or prayed, or sat on a rock overlooking the city of Jerusalem. Christ must have come up here hundreds of times, and spent hundreds of hours in prayer. Here is where Jesus prayed for the world and for the peace of Jerusalem.

every day, that prayer to his Father was the center of his life. That's why they asked him to teach them to pray as he prayed.

On Olivet I met especially the mystery of Christ's loneliness. Nobody really understood who he was, or what his life was all about. Mary understood some, but she was still a creature. Only the Father knew.

One of Catherine's themes in her own spiritual life is her passion to assuage the loneliness of Christ. "Christ is in pain until the end of time," wrote Peguy. She has an intuition from the Spirit (which is perfectly in keeping with the theology of the Church) that in some real way the sufferings of Christ -- and hence also his loneliness -- continues on in his Body which is the Church. If the Body suffers, the Head who is joined to the Body must somehow share in that suffering. "Saul, Saul, why are you persecuting Me ? St. Augustine says, "He did not say "Why are you persecuting my Body ? ' but 'Why are you persecuting Me ?' "

In a sermon for the feast of the Ascension, Augustine wrote:

> For just as he remained with us after his ascension, so we too are already in heaven with him, even though what is promised us has not yet been fulfilled in our bodies.
>
> Christ is exalted above the heavens, but he still suffers on earth all the pain that we, the members of his body, have to bear. While in heaven he is also with us, and we while on earth

are with him. These words are explained by our oneness with Christ, for he is our head and we are his body.

You can conceive of this mystery in several ways: 1) When Christ was on earth he suffered (and knew about) the sufferings of all peoples of all times; 2) Through the doctrine of the Mystical Body he continues to suffer now what his Body suffers. It's a deep mystery; we can't explain it. But it is a truth of our faith that in some real way we are "making up in our bodies what is wanting in the sufferings of Christ," and that we (Head and members) share now the same glories and sorrows.

This desire to assuage the loneliness of Christ was part of my spiritual life even before I came to Madonna House. A poem by E.E. Cummings says it powerfully:

> No time ago
> Or else a life,
> Walking in the dark
> I met Christ Jesus.
> He was as close as
> I am to you -- no, closer.
> Made of nothing, except loneliness.

"Made of loneliness." An open wound of loneliness. A divine loneliness that no human person can assuage. Several times in Gethsemane Jesus sought out his disciples. He knew they couldn't take away his loneliness and dread. He just wanted some human companionship, that's all. Many sufferings are like that. We can't really do anything for people, but it helps if somebody is just *there*. Perhaps that's all we can do with Christ in his loneliness. How it would give comfort to his Heart!

I walked many hours with the lonely Christ up and down the paths of the Mount of Olives, wishing I could love more so as to console him more.

The next day was Friday, October 21. During my night vigil it came to me strongly that on my pilgrimage I should be praying for all the pilgrims who are not praying. I had been toying with the idea of visiting St. Catherine's monastery on Mt. Sinai, but decided against it. The only way to get there is on a tour. I didn't look forward to four days on a tour without time for prayer. Besides, I would be seeing plenty of monasteries on Mt. Athos.

I set out early that day and walked completely around the walls of the Old City. Then, at the Christian Information Centre, I arranged to celebrate Mass one morning in the Church of the Holy Sepulchre. I was hesitant to arrange too many other Masses. The Lord had already provided me with a celebration at Gethsemane. I would trust him to get me in on other celebrations as well.

There was more on the Mount of Olives I hadn't seen. I had visited the Church called Peter in Gallicantu where Peter wept over the denial of his Master. Here I prayed for the gift of tears for my own sins. At the Church call Dominus Flevit, where Christ wept over Jerusalem, I prayed for the gift of tears to weep over the sins of others, the multitude of sins which in some way continues to make Christ weep.

To my regret, the Russian monastery of the Ascension on the Mount of Olives was closed, and I never did get in. Near the top of Olivet I visited the Evangelical Sisters of Mary, the group founded by Basileia Schlink. The superior *looked like* Mother Basileia, with a radiant and joyful face. We had a pleasant visit together, complete with a cool drink after my long climb.

I also visited the Benedictine monastery nearby. I bought a beautiful, original icon of our Lady of Tenderness, the one where the Infant is cheek to cheek with our Lady. My twin sister Andrea has a House of Prayer in Ohio, and I thought this would be a nice gift for her chapel. She calls her House "Marian Solitude." I also bought many small wooden rosaries.

That evening I had the liturgy at Ecce Home for the Sisters and guests. I told them of four experiences I had had already which had become for me symbols of deeper realities. Three of them I have already mentioned: The Ethiopian monk was a symbol of the hunger Christians have for unity; the beauty behind closed doors was a symbol of the beauty within each of us, often hidden behind drab appearances; "What's this, George?" was a symbol of how superficial we Christians are and can be about our faith.

The fourth symbol/experience I have not mentioned yet. Ecce Homo is in the Moslem quarter of the Old City. There are regular calls to prayer over the loud speakers, day and night (4 A.M.!) The very first time I heard that call to prayer I thought to myself: "It sounds so *sad.*" It always sounded to me like a cry for Someone, Someone who was not present – a cry for Christ. Each time I heard that call I prayed that some day the Moslems would come to believe in Christ as Messiah and God.

Today there is a strong current of thought to recognize what is good in non-Christian religions; this is encouraged by the Vatican Council itself. There is much dialoguing going on not only among Christians, but among Christians and far-Eastern religions as well. A lesser known movement is what Luke Malik calls the "New Ecumenism," embracing Jews, Christians, and Moslems. Each of these great traditions believe that we are all children of one father, Abraham, and brothers and sisters to one another. Surely this movement towards unity is a work of the Holy Spirit in our day, and is to be encouraged.

But whenever I would walk out onto the roof overlooking the Old City and see the Mosque of Omar sacred to the Muslims, I would think to myself: "Christ also weeps over the Mosque of Omar." Yes, many of the obstacles to unity have been caused by the sins of Christians and their lack of fidelity to the Gospel. But there is a more fundamental disbelief which Christ encountered before the sins of Christians, a basic resistance to him that is part of original sin itself, and cannot be blamed on the specific sins of Christians towards Jews and Muslims. Whatever blinds people to Christ as the Messiah, as the Son of God, is a cause for Christ's weeping.

Christians have sinned historically in trying to *make* people believe in Christ. Only the Spirit of God can convert people to Christ. The task of the Christian is to witness to the love of Christ; then Christ will do the rest. The point is that there is a fundamental blindness *in human nature itself* to Christ as Messiah; which is prior to our present divisions and the added obstacles to belief present in those divisions. Enormous as the crimes by Christians against Jews have been, we cannot allow this to distort Christ's vision for all peoples. The greatest act of love we can perform towards anyone, of whatever faith or race or nationality, is to desire that that person believe in Jesus Christ as the Saviour of the world. This is the Father's plan.

We can go too far in emphasizing what is good in other religions. Judaism and Buddhism and Hinduism existed before the sins of Christians. We presume Jesus came because none of these religions were good enough, and this is still true. To desire that the Jewish and Muslem peoples believe in Jesus is not anti-Jewish or anti-Muslem. It is simply our belief in God the Father's saving plan for the world.

On my pilgrimage I was overwhelmed by the world's rejection of Christ: God become a Man and we did not recognize who he was. Thus, I couldn't reconcile going to see the Mosque of Omar with what God was doing in my heart. Christ on the Mount of Olives was not just weeping over his own Jewish people. He was weeping over the blindness of the whole world.

Along the Via Dolorosa, not far from Ecce Homo, is the prison where Christ was kept overnight. The Greek Orthodox watch over this holy place. Every prison in every age is bad enough, but what must the prisons in those days have been like! Not more than holes in the ground. I descended the stairs and sat in this place where Christ had been held prisoner.

Christ as Prisoner! He really identified with us in everything. This cave was one of the lowest geographical levels of Christ's "descent" into our world: He descended right into our foul and stinking prisons. I guess I never thought much about his being a Prisoner, never having been one myself. I'm sure many prisoners have meditated on this mystery.

Christ as Prisoner! Here he sat -- bound, guarded, caged in – and yet he remained the supremely Free One. By becoming a Prisoner, Christ has set all prisoners free, if only they believe in him. Bound and restricted externally, Jesus was free; so too, prisoners, even in solitary confinement, can become perfectly free if they give their freedom to Christ. If we believe in Christ, we are free, no matter what external bondage we are under.

This prison was dark and hopeless; yet it was filled with the Light of the world, filled with hosts of angels who, at his word, could have blasted the doors and iron bars just as they did for Peter. But their power was restrained. Instead, they worshipped in awe the Prisoner who was setting all prisoners free.

There is a lower prison called the "Prison of Barrabas" where the hard-core prisoners were kept. Dismas was there also. If only all prisoners who are justly in prison for their crimes could believe that Christ is there with them, just as he was that night with Dismas. I believe the presence of Christ in prison that night began to work in the heart of Dismas even before his choice on Calvary. Death was approaching on the morrow. Dismas was thinking about his relationship with his God, how it would go with him. No prisoner need despair. Like Dismas, their prison can become a meeting place with Christ. And, as far as we know, it was a prisoner who was one of the first to enter into paradise which had been closed to us. If a thief and a criminal like Dismas can get into paradise through one act of faith, we should all have immense confidence in God's mercy. What magnificent words Jesus spoke to him: "This day you shall be with me in paradise."

We have had recently an outstanding modern image of the presence of Christ in prisons -- Pope John Paul's visit to the man who attempted to assassinate him. By going himself, the Pope became an icon of the forgiving presence of Christ who is always in all the prisons of the world. Many prisoners might have said to themselves. "Oh, if only the Pope could visit us too." *Christ is with you.* That's what the visit of the Pope means. God allowed himself to be put in chains so he could break the interior chains of all prisoners. what a wonderful God we have who identified with us in all our miseries so as to set us free from them all!.

CHAPTER FOUR
Jerusalem : Cenacle, Emmaus, Mass at the Holy Sepulchre

The Cenacle, or Upper Room, is, for us Christians, the second holiest place on earth after the Holy Sepulchre. Here the first Eucharist was celebrated. Here was the meeting place of the first Church — Mary, the Apostles, and the first followers of Jesus. Here Jesus appeared to his Apostles after his Resurrection. Here the Holy Spirit descended upon the infant Church. Here the Apostles and disciples continued to gather for their meetings and fellowship, the Council of Jerusalem, for example. From this room the Good News spread to the known ends of the world. Surely one of the holiest places on earth.

I knew very little about the Cenacle, so I matter-of-factly expected to find a shrine of some kind, decorations, vigil lights, icons and paintings, many symbols of the astounding events I have just enumerated.

There was nothing, absolutely nothing of the kind ! I went in and out of the actual Cenacle several times, thinking that I must surely have the wrong place. When I finally discovered I was indeed in the Cenacle, I was overcome with a flood of powerful emotions (which is rare for me). I was confused, hurt, angry, bewildered, sad, shocked -- all at the same time. There was absolutely nothing here ! Not one Christian symbol, not one picture, not one vigil light. Nothing, absolutely nothing !

I found a stone block (there are not even chairs or benches to sit on) and just sat there for two hours. Now *I* was guilty of saying what that young man said in the Cave of Bethlehem: "Is this it ? " Here of all places one really needed to exercise pure faith. On one of the upper portions of a column there is a mother pelican feeding her starving offspring with her blood; this was a cherished Eucharistic symbol from Crusader times. This is the only Christian symbol. The only other are Muslim, left over from the time when this room had been used for centuries as a mosque. Everything elso is bare, and not even clean at that. If I had had the gift of tears, I would have wept here. Who is responsible for this ? Why this barrenness and nakedness ? Why, why Lord in such a holy place ?

I was to return here several times, but I must admit that on this first occasion I was unable to really pray or enter into the Presence. The shock was too profound. If I prayed, I prayed against the attitudes and forces which had conspired to keep this place in such a state. I prayed that the walls of prejudice would come down forever. I sat there in sadness because Christ is still not accepted, still not believed in by his own people.

For I was on Mount Zion. Down below was David's tomb. Adjacent to the Cenacle, in the same complex of buildings actually, was a Yeshiva, a school for the study of Torah. The Christians did not own this building, and thus had no say over the up-keep of the Cenacle. The drabness of the Cenacle was a dramatic symbol for me of the rejection of Christ. He was not welcome here.
"He came unto his own and his own did not know who he was."

I'm not thinking only of the Jewish people: most of the world still does not believe in Christ as God come among us. This is the greatest tragedy in the world. All others flow from the failure to believe in this Man.

On this first visit I did manage to be grateful for the immense gift of the Eucharist and of my priesthood. Here also the tours are rushing in and out. One wonders why they come.

I left, and walked to the sacred Wailing Wall of the Jewish people which is not far from the Cenacle. Mary, a young Christian friend of mine who was beginning to appreciate the Jewish roots of the Gospel, had asked me to put a prayer in the Wall for her as is the custom. You write a prayer on a piece of paper and insert it into one of the cracks.

It is very inspiring to see the reverence with which people approach and pray at this Wall. I know this is again going against much modern thinking, but I prayed at that Wall for the conversion of the Jewish people to Christ. The Father wants all his children to listen to his Son. On only two occasions in the New Testament do we hear the Father speak, at the Baptism and Transfiguration of Christ. On both occasions the Father says the same thing: "This is my beloved Son. Listen to him." This is the cure for every evil in the world. What else is there to pray for?

I prayed for all the Jewish people I knew who had been converted to Christ, and thus entered into the fullness of their biblical promises. I prayed for Miriam and Robert and François. I prayed for a Jewish young man I had met early in my life who had described to me how, after becoming a Christian, he had to step over his mother's body to get out of his ancestral home. I asked pardon of God for all the sins of Christians against the Jews. Forgiveness is the only answer.

The Benedictine Abbey of the Dormition of our Lady is also on Mount Zion. Downstairs is a beautiful shrine to her "falling asleep." I prayed for a happy death for myself and all my loved ones. I was glad to see a mosaic of our Lady of Guadalupe there.

The next day, my first Sunday in the Holy Land, I thought I would try to visit three places where the resurrection appearances occurred. I was successful. I walked first to the Holy Sepulchre (I always had trouble finding it). The Coptic liturgy was being celebrated. I prayed with them for fifteen minutes or so, never having prayed with Coptic brothers and sisters before. Perhaps thirty or forty people were present. Only the men and the priests were singing, and very loud. I wondered if all the others present knew what was being said or sung.

Then I attended several hours of the splendid Greek Orthodox Liturgy. Again, not many people were present; two scholas of boys, led by a cantor, were doing all the singing. The Patriarch was there because in a few days a special celebration of his feast day was planned. I didn't go to Communion, but did go up and receive the antidoron. This is blessed bread given out at the end of the service. Then I made my way to the Cenacle again.

Ever since my first painful visit to the Cenacle, and, since I had learned from a priest at

The Cenacle was a large, sad, empty room. I united with my brothers who do not have the freedom to celebrate the Eucharist openly in the light of day.

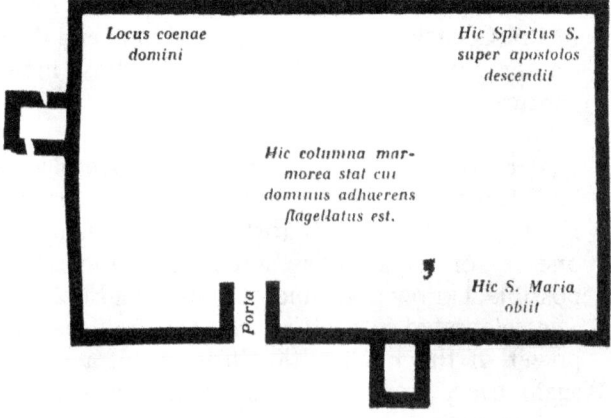

The Upper Room commemorates the Eucharist, the Priesthood, the Descent of the Holy Spirit, the death of Mary, the Mandatum, the sacrament of Penance, the witness of Thomas and the infant church. In the past, the column of the flagellation was venerated here; today it is in the Franciscan chapel of the Basilica of the Holy Sepulcher.

the Abbey that no Christian services were allowed in the Cenacle, a desire grew in me to celebrate the Eucharist there. Here of all places where the Eucharist was first given to us; here where the early Christians gathered to share the Holy Meal; here of all places the power of the Eucharist should radiate. Hence, when I prayed in the Cenacle today, I meditated long and deep on the Eucharist which took place those many centuries ago.

In our Catholic theology we have always had what is called "spiritual Communion," reception of the Eucharist in spirit when, for one reason or another, actual reception is not possible. I know that sunday morning a Eucharist was celebrated in the Cenacle. I desired that the power of the Eucharistic Christ penetrate once again every nook and cranny of this room. I desired that once again the words "This is my Body ...this is my Blood" resound within those walls and re-consecrate and re-dedicate everything.

I spent an hour or so in this way. My thoughts also turned to the Church in persecuted countries, to Eucharists taking place at this very hour clandestinely in prison camps, basements, and tightly-guarded rooms of all kinds. I united with my brothers and sisters who do not have the freedom to celebrate the Eucharist openly in the light of day.

A friend of mine, Lorne, had given me a reference on Mt. Sion, the name of a Jewish teacher at one of the Yeshivas. I thought, while I was here, I would look him up.

I approached a building in order to make an inquiry. Two Jewish men were sitting outside.

One saw my icon and said: "Don't come in here with that thing on ! Hide it or take it off !"

Well, I was prepared to do neither, so I just smiled, said "God bless you," and started to walk away. Just a few moments later another man came up to me and asked if he could help. I said yes, and told him the name of the man I was looking for. He said, "Follow me."

What a painful encounter with that first gentleman ! What or whom was he reacting to ? He wasn't relating to me; he doesn't know me. Was he relating to my Christ ? He doesn't know him either, since He's the most wonderful Person who ever lived. Was he relating to history, to his past, to his own hurts ? What ? What an unreal encounter that was !

As I was now following this other man I thought to myself: We must meet each other person to person. We can't meet types or history or bad memories. We have to meet each other, persons. It's the only way out of prejudice and the sins of our ancestors.

In the space of two minutes I encountered a rather hostile Jewish person and a wonderfully friendly one. It's the same with every other "class" or "group." I met Israeli soldiers who would hardly look at me; I met Israeli soldiers who spontaneously offered me rides and helped me make long-distance phone calls. I met Orthodox priests who were quite cold and distant; I met an Orthodox priest who spent twenty minutes with me in pleasant conversation. If only we could always deal with real people and not with abstract groups... I was sad that that young man at the entrance a few minutes ago did not meet me as a person. Lord have mercy on me for all the times I've done that, for all the times my ancestors have done that to the Jews.

A few moments later I was introduced to the man I was looking for. I thanked my guide with especial gratitude. I then spent fifteen minutes chatting pleasantly with this man who turned out to be a teacher at the Yeshiva. He was very open, kind and warm.

The conversation turned to the tours, and how people rush by the holy places. He said the Jews do the same thing. This used to bother him but then he thought that when the tourists went back to their rooms at night, and to their homes eventually, they did reflect upon their experiences, and profit from them. I said I hope so. We shook hands and parted.

This was my only real encounter with a Jewish teacher of any kind. I was glad I had looked him up. Glad too, in another way, for my first painful encounter. It was a small taste of the pain of Jewish-Christian relations on holy Mount Zion.

EMMAUS

My third resurrection stop that day was Emmaus. Idealistically, of course, I thought of walking, like the disciples. But the day was moving on, and I had no idea of how to get there. So I took a taxi. When I arrived the gate was closed, but I rang the bell anyway. A gracious Franciscan friar (who turned out to be from Montreal) opened the gate when he learned who I was and where I was from. Since it was the off-time, the grounds were very peaceful and quiet. I asked if I could celebrate Mass, and he said I could.

There are several altars in the basilica. I must have read something from a brochure (I don't remember), but as I entered the church my eye turned immediately to the altar on the north side. Sure enough, this was the altar of St. Cleophas, built on the foundations of a house "evidently which existed before the Crusaders' church was built, and ... seems to be about 2,000 years old." This was the altar I chose for Mass.

I was all alone in the church; it was Sunday afternoon. Was it about the same time the Lord had his meal with the disciples ? Now, I was eating this Eucharistic meal with Jesus who so graciously met and walked with his friends, and ate that beautiful meal with them.

One of the graces of this visit was becoming better acquainted with these friends, or rather relatives, of Jesus.

Many biblical scholars assert the following: 1) that Cleophas was the brother of St. Joseph as well as Mary's cousin; hence he was Jesus' uncle and Mary's brother-in-law; 2) that Mary of Cleophas at the foot of the Cross (John 19:25) was this man's wife; 3) that they had four illustrious sons: James the Less (Matt.4:21), the first bishop of Jerusalem; Joseph called Barsabbas (Acts 1:23), a candidate with Matthias to replace Judas; Judas Thaddeus (Acts 1:13) one of the Twelve Apostles; Simeon, one of the seventy-two disciples, who was the second bishop of Jerusalem. Also, most ancient historians consider Salome as the eldest daughter of

Cleophas. More questionable is the opinion that another Mary in the Gospel was also a daughter of Cleophas. The remark in the brochure here is worth quoting:

> It certainly is a comforting surprise to know that St. Cleophas, disciple and relative of Christ, was at the head of a family of faithful followers of the Lord. Thus we may say that, after the Holy Family of Nazareth, the Family of Cleophas of Emmaus should be considered a model for Christian family life.

Walking around the lovely grounds that afternoon I had the impression that I was in a home atmosphere where Jesus must have often come to relax and be refreshed by people who loved him and understood him. I was to receive a similar gift.

I was coming out of the front door of the chapel when the Franciscan superior came walking towards me. As he approached I said to myself, "I think I know him." He was the first to come forth with the name: "Bob Wild!" *His* name did not come as quickly, but I had been with him in the Franciscan seminary twenty-nine years ago! As I said, it was a special gift from the Lord to meet a friend of my own at the house of friends of Jesus.

It was a joyful reunion. Father Raphael gave me the grand tour, and then invited me for supper with the friars.

I don't know why, but the word I received at Emmaus was "holy conversation." Maybe it flowed from the happy conversations I had with

My third Resurrection stop that Sunday was Emmaus.

There are several altars in the Basilica. I must have read something from a brochure (I don't remember), but as I entered the church my eye turned immediately to the altar on the north side. Sure enough, this was the altar of St. Cleophas.

At Emmaus, the Latin words over the gate mean "Lord, stay with us".

Father Raphael; I'm sure it flowed also from my meditations on the Gospel story of Emmaus. Along the road, their sadness was turned into joy by the presence and holy conversation of Jesus who consoled and explained the scriptures to them. And then, what a joy to sit down with him at table and listen to his gracious speech.

My prayer was that the risen Christ would always anoint my speech, that my words would console and bring hope to people, and break for them the bread of the scriptures.

My second grace was somehow becoming a part of Cleophas' family. They became my new brothers and sisters, these apostles and disciples and bishops and martyrs, and holy women who were friends of Mary. Imagine them all together in this house, sitting around a table and discussing the Lord Jesus. I acquired some new friends that day. Being in their home brought Christ's humanity closer to me also: he too enjoyed a visit with his friends.

Mass at the Holy Sepulchre

The next day, Monday, proved to be the high-point of my pilgrimage. I was scheduled to celebrate Mass in the Holy Sepulchre Church at 5:30 a.m. I chose that early hour for at least one obvious reason: Jesus rose early in the morning. But also very few people - especially tours - are around early in the morning. It would be quiet and peaceful.

In preparation I knelt before the Crucifix on Mt. Calvary - but not for long. I was thinking ahead about my Mass when I suddenly discovered that I had forgotten my little ticket (cartula) stating my time and day. You can't celebrate without it. Even though I was on Mount Calvary, I panicked. I practically ran down the stairs to find the Franciscan Father in charge. I suppose I could have run back to Ecce Homo and get it if need be. Did I have time ? Oh no! Don't tell me I'm going to miss celebrating Mass here at the Center of Christianity !

I found the priest in charge. Trying to remain calm, but obviously not, I said, as honestly as I could: "Father, I'm scheduled to celebrate Mass here this morning, but I forgot my ticket." I held my breath. Would I get a hard line or a soft line ? God, help me ! The priest didn't seem too upset. It seems it has happened before. He said: "No problem, as long as somebody else doesn't come with a ticket." Thank you, Lord. what a relief.

There is a Latin chapel in the church of the Sepulchre. I had been there and seen priests celebrating Mass. I thought that's where I would be going too. As I was vesting the priest said, rather nonchalantly, "You're going into the Holy Sepulchre." I said, "What ?" He said, "You're going into the Holy Sepulchre to celebrate Mass. You have a half-hour."

Going *into* the Holy Sepulchre ! I didn't even know they did that. I hadn't seen any Eucharist celebrated in there since I arrived. I wasn't prepared for this. My whole being started swimming around. "Going *into* the Holy Sepulchre. Going to celebrate Mass *in the tomb of Christ*, right *in* the tomb." All I could think of taking with me was the packet of intentions and a little silver chalice I had bought to place on every altar where I celebrated Mass. Two minutes later the priest was escorting me into the tomb.

91

Everything was arranged. A wooden pallet had been placed over the tomb and on it was arranged all the necessary things for Mass. He reminded me once again of the time limit, and left. And there I was, standing in my priestly vestments in front of the tomb of Christ. Two Sisters from the Phillipines saw me enter and came in to celebrate with me. (Like the women in the Garden.)

I am not usually discombobulated, but for the next half-hour I was really in another world. The suddenness of it all was too much. Again, I wasn't prepared. But here I was. I think I said and did all the proper things for Mass, but I wouldn't bet on it. All I could think of was the risen Christ, that here is where my Christ burst forth from the tomb; and here I was, celebrating right on his tomb the everlasting memorial of that fact.

I went through the gestures; I remember distinctly praying for my parents and family. I put my packets of intentions on the altar and lifted all those people up to Christ. I pronounced the sacred words; we ate the Sacred Food. I'm sure the Sisters were as ecstatic as I.

You can't be "recollected" at a time like that. You're in a state beyond recollection, at least I was. All I could think of was Jesus, Jesus risen from the dead, Jesus now filling the whole universe. Everything was Jesus. There was nothing and no one else for that whole half-hour. I understood a little the words of the Evangelist describing the Mount Tabor experience: "They saw only Jesus." Maybe heaven will be simply an intensification of this consciousness: our minds and hearts will be inundated with Jesus, and nothing else. I believe it was one of the most sublime experiences of my whole life -- certainly the holiest of my pilgrimage.

I had walked into the tomb in a daze, been there in a daze, and I walked out in a daze. I mechanically took off my vestments and thanked the priest. Your state, after such an experience, is also beyond thanksgiving. How do you say "thank you" for that ? So I just went and sat in front of the open tomb, just sat there. In some real, spiritual way, I had seen the risen Christ.

I went back up to Calvary to continue my meditations. As I arrived, a Latin High Mass began in the Sepulchre below. The ancient Latin phrases – "Gloria in Excelsis Deo -- Credo in unum Deum... Agnus Dei" -- were beautiful. If only we all were united – Jews, Muslims, Orthodox, Latins -- we could pool all our aesthetic talents and traditions and create a harmonious liturgy truly representative of all mankind which would astound even the angels. Each tradition has its own beauty. Surely it's God's plan that all the artistry in the world, all the creativity in the world, purified from sin and blindness, converge to glorify his Son, his Beloved One. At present, all the colors of our creative rainbow are fragmented. What beauty if they were all blended together !

This was my third time on Calvary. Already some of the consciousness of its holiness was beginning to wear off. How dull we are ! How quickly we become "used to" the Holy in a bad sense. The first day we are on our knees; the next day we just hurry up the sacred stairs like any other stairs, or almost.

Afterwards I went to a little restaurant for some breakfast. A decently dressed, English-speaking man was already sitting in one of the booths. After I sat down he came over and asked for a dime for a cup of coffee. He was obviously an alcoholic. Being still so filled with the presence of the risen Christ, I couldn't say anything but, "Please sit down." We had breakfast together. He wasn't a practicing christian, but had been born in the church. I recognized Christ in him. I hope he met Christ in a new way again in me.

That afternoon I decided to spend more time on the Mount of Olives. As I was walking there a Muslim boy approached along the Via Dolorosa, saw my icon, and said, "Who's that?" I'm sure he knew. I said, "Jesus, God, Saviour." He said "For us, God up there," pointing to the sky. I said, "For us, God up there come down here," also making the appropriate gestures. He smiled. He knew what I meant.

I stopped again at the tomb of our Lady. On the way out I met a young Orthodox monk who was tending the shrine. He hadn't been there on my previous visit. He saw my icon and asked if I was Orthodox. I said no, a Roman Catholic priest, but I love the Orthodox. He smiled. Turns out he was a monk from St. Catherine's monastery on Mt. Sinai; also, he had spent some time on Athos. I was getting closer.

It wasn't exactly a conversation we had; I listened mostly. He obviously wanted to make a few points. He saw my small wooden Jesus beads and said "that's only wood." Then he went on to describe some of the symbolism of the chotki he himself was using. He said each cloth bead was made up of nine crosses, one for each of the nine (I helped him with the next word) choirs of angels. Then I said: "But the important think is not the rosary but the purity of prayer one says on a rosary." He smiled and said yes.

He started talking about how loosely we are using the word "church" these days. He said for him there is only one church, the Church which goes back to the Fathers.

I told him I was going to visit Mount Athos. He said he had been there several times. He said, "You might not come back!" I said I would because "too many people are praying that I come back, and their prayers are very powerful." We blessed each other and parted. Nice guy.

Again in the evening I spent several hours walking and praying on the Mount of Olives. I met a delightful Arab gentleman who invited me to come sometime and have coffee with him. He lived nearby. I said I would. I told him I was hoping to go to Bethlehem tomorrow. He said if it were not for the elections tomorrow, he would take me. I did return to his house for coffee a few days later. Another one of those gifts which come from simply walking prayerfully around holy places.

When I returned that night to Ecce Homo, and went up on the roof to get some night air, I was greeted by a startling new symbol. There, on top of the Church of the Holy Sepulchre, was a huge, glowing, white electric cross shining splendidly over the whole city. It was a magnificent sight ! I learned afterwards it was in honor of the Greek Patriarch's feast day. Oh, if only everyone believed in Christ, and the dominance of that brilliant Cross was a reality in all the cities and hearts of the earth! May it soon be so ! May it soon be so !

CHAPTER FIVE
BETHLEHEM

Around ten o'clock I took a sherut to Bethlehem. As you're driving down these roads you can't help think of the Holy Family walking. We arrived in the central square, near the Basilica. The first thing I always needed to do was just soak up the atmosphere. So I sat down at one of the outdoor tables, ordered a little lunch, and allowed the fact that I was in Bethlehem sink in.

As I was watching the hustle and bustle of the market place, watching the beautiful Arab girls and handsome men go by, the thought came to me: at a certain point in time, God simply chose one these girls and one these men, and involved them in the greatest drama in the history of the world – the coming of his Son, the Messiah. Imagine having it gradually dawn on Mary and Joseph that they were the main characters of this event of all events.

By faith and love each of us can assume a greater and greater part in this ongoing drama, if we want to. I think the saints were people who wanted to take part in this drama with all their hearts, with all their talents. They too, after a while, found themselves as important actors and actresses in the story. I think we have too predetermined a notion of how God chooses people for roles in his love story. There are special characters, of course, like Mary and Joseph. But I think we could all have very major parts if we had the courage to get onto the stage. Nobody is really called to sit in the wings and watch.

Accommodations had been arranged for me at the Franciscan Sisters of Mary on top of the hill behind the Basilica. As I was walking up Milk Grotto Road I approached a small group of school girls to ask where the convent was. One of the girls, seeing my icon, ran up to me, kissed her hand, and touched my icon! It was a lovely, spontaneous gesture, the most faith-filled reverencing of my icon since I left Combermere. Appropriately enough it was done by a child in the city of children, Bethlehem. Only someone with a childlike heart could do what she did. It moved me deeply; I felt at home.

I had a most pleasant room in the convent over-looking the city. It was complete with an icon of the Nativity. After getting settled and resting a bit I decided, of course that my very first stop would be the Cave where Christ was born.

I would say that, after the Holy Sepulchre, the Cave of Bethlehem was a high-point of my pilgrimage. My journey was in thanksgiving for the coming of the Redeemer, and here is where he first appeared, although in a hidden, quiet, almost shy way.

The ancient world thought the cosmos was composed of four basic elements - air, water, fire, and earth. One of my meditations had to do with how Christ, by his coming, had sanctified each of these elements.

Bethlehem is where he took his first breath of air, and so here is where all the air was sanctified. When he descended into the Jordan River to be baptized, he sanctified all the waters of the earth, as the Eastern Liturgy of the feast so well describes. And some of the Fathers say that when he was buried in the earth, he sanctified all the earth. I have my own explana-

I would say that after the Holy Sepulcher the Cave of Bethlehem was a highpoint of my pilgrimage.

tion for the last element, fire: he sanctified all the fire when the Holy Spirit came down in tongues of fire at Pentecost.

It was here, kneeling before the crib of the Child, watching the tours rapidly come and go, that I noted down in my diary I would try to write a book and do what I could to offset the spirit of tourism at the holy places. Maybe it was because of the quietness of the Cave; maybe it was the romance of Bethlehem; maybe it was the sanctity of the place where the Word became flesh and began living among us – I don't know – but here, more than anywhere else, the tourist attitude "got to me."

On entering the Cave, the first thing so many people did – before prayer, before anything else -- was to take pictures. Cameras are a bane for pilgrims. As is often the case when we encounter the Holy, we look around frantically for some distraction. Cameras provide one such distraction, one such escape, from the Holy. We know the Holy is there, but it's as though we must look at God sideways, unable to gaze upon him directly with "unveiled faces." Really, it's as if people pretend the Holy Place is not there at all.

After a couple of hours of prayer in the Cave I took a walk to find the Shepherd's Field. On the way one of the shopkeepers saw my icon and said, "Nice ! Want to sell it ?" I said, "No, it's not for sale. It's my pilgrim icon." "Greek ?" he asked. "No, it's Russian." "Nice."

I didn't actually get to the Field that afternoon, but I saw a great deal of Beit Sahur, a little town near Bethlehem. Just by walking around you can drink in much of the atmosphere.

It seemed at one point I was heading out into the desert. I was ! A Jewish man stopped of his own accord and asked if I needed a ride. I said I didn't know, as I wasn't sure where I was going. Turns out I was going nowhere. It was getting on towards dusk, so I headed back towards Bethlehem.

I got lost here as well. I spied a man on crutches and stopped to ask directions. He spoke fairly good English. When he found out I was a priest from Canada he invited me into his home to meet his family and have some coffee. I accepted.

Most of Beit Sahur is Christian. They knew all about Archbishop Raya and were delighted to know I knew him. I had a very pleasant visit with Joseph and his family. Joseph's brother-in-law stopped in. He was the principal at a local school and also spoke fairly good English.

Before I left I enquired about Joseph's leg. Seems he had had an accident. I asked if he wanted me to pray over him for healing. He said he did, so I prayed over him. He had given me hospitality, so I wanted to give him something in return. His brother-in-law then drove me to within a short distance of Bethlehem.

A Maccabee beer at the local Inn. Supper at the convent. Correspondence. And so to bed. End of Day One in the city of David.

THE MILK GROTTO

The convent where I was staying was on Milk Grotto Road, so named because Mary stopped here to breast-feed the Child on the way to Egypt. This was my first stop the next day.

There were at least a dozen paintings in the church from a variety of traditions depicting Mary giving suck to the Child. Coming from my "proper" North American culture I don't think I had ever seen a picture of Mary breast-feeding the Child. I copied down some of the scripture quotes from the walls and under the pictures, because they led me into different aspects of the mystery of our Lady's place in the Church.

Mary is the Mother of the Church. However, I had never seen applied to her this text from Isaiah: "Oh, that you may suck fully at the milk of her comfort, that you may nurse with delight at her abundant breasts" (66:11). Freudians (unfortunately) would have a field day with this one: Christians nursing themselves at the breasts of our Lady !

There is a profound spiritual sense in which this is perfectly true. St. Peter says: "Be as eager for milk as newborn babies – pure milk of the spirit to make you grow into salvation, now that you have tasted that the Lord is good" (2:2-3). We are God's children. One of our deepest nourishments is to be fed by our Lady, by our personal relationship with her as Mother of Christ. I prayed here for all those struggling with devotion to Mary, those who have been turned off for the wrong reasons. She herself says to each of us, again in the words of Isaiah: "All you who are thirsty, come to the water. You who have no money, come, receive grain and eat; come, without paying and without cost, drink wine and milk" (55:1). It must be a great sadness for the Mother of God that she cannot pour out her maternal care on all her children. The "children" have become too sophisticated to drink milk from her breasts.

It occured to me also here that Mary was a refugee, so she is our Lady of Refugees as well; and there are so many millions today.

As I was sitting, praying in the shrine, I saw some women come in, dip their fingers in the oil of the vigil lights, and touch their breasts. There was an inscription, so I went over and read it. It is believed that the oil from the lamps burning before the breast-feeding Madonna is a blessing against breast cancer. I prayed for Marian, a dear friend of mine who had had both of her breasts removed years ago. I put some oil on my breasts too !

Another friend of mine, Mary, used to be very involved in La Leche League, an organization to reintroduce natural breast-feeding among mothers. I remembered the first time I saw natural breast-feeding. It was while on a visit to a family here in Combermere. A mother was holding her child and, at a certain point, she simply exposed one of her breasts and began feeding her child. I couldn't help watching ! I could see that such a practice could help lessen men's preoccupation with womens' breasts. After you've watched a naked breast feed a child in parlor for twenty minutes, it doesn't become a preoccupation any more. Mary, give us pure hearts about our bodies.

MONASTERY OF ST. THEODOSIUS

This was to be a particularly exciting day for me because for the first time I would be touching some of the most ancient monastic settlements in the world. My next stop was to be the monastery of the great "cenobiarch" Theodosius.

He was born in Cappadocia in 424 and entered the monastic life at an early age. Around 475, between Bethlehem and the monastery of St. Sabas (which I also hoped to visit), he established a great monastery of over four hundred monks of different nationalities. He also founded a home for the aged and the poor, and a vocational school. He died in the 529 at the age of one hundred and four!

Besides my personal interest in monasticism these monasteries were significant to me for another reason. According to Fedotov (*The Russian Religious Mind*) Russian monasticism, and hence much of Russian spirituality, was profoundly influenced by the Palestinian concept of the Christian life. The Russian Theodosius, who, along with St. Anthony, was the founder of the famous Caves Monastery of Kiev, was named after the Palestinian Theodosius. and just as the latter included vast charities to the poor as part of his concept and practice of monastic life, so Theodosius the Russian made works of charity part of his christian monastic life-style. This was a marked departure from much Egyptian and Greek monasticism.

I mention this because Theodosius the Russian became *the model* of the Christian for the Russians, and Catherine Doherty carries on that tradition in her formation of our Madonna House community. So, at the monastery of Theodosius in Palestine, I was coming home to one of the deep sources of Catherine's spirituality.

I took a taxi to the Holy Trinity Monastery of Theodosius. (Not exactly a long trek through the desert. But that would come.) The driver dropped me off ten feet in front of the large iron gates. I pulled the bell rope and waited. An

Orthodox nun opened. I asked if I could come in and see the church. She opened the gate and led me into a little courtyard. As I hesitated, she motioned me further into the magnificent church.

I am not given to exaggeration, but there must have been at least a hundred icons in there. I was overwhelmed with a sense of really being in the presence of heavenly beings – of being in heaven, actually. This would be the first of many similar experiences. I began reverencing the icons, especially the ancient ones of Theodosius. Then I prostrated on the floor and prayed. My mind and heart were flooded with all the tales of the monks I had ever read. What a holy place I was in ! How many hundreds of thousands of hours of prayer have ascended to the Lord Christ from this holy ground ! Oh, I just wanted to stay here for hours.

It was not to be. The nun was nervous. She began making noises in the back of the church. Finally, after about twenty minutes, she came over to me and motioned that it was time to leave. Too bad. It would have been spiritually delicious just to sit in the church, or in the little courtyard, and soak up the presences of the centuries.

I kissed the holy images of Theodosius once more, gave the nun a donation, thanked her, and left. It was a brief visit, but very holy. "Your abundant tears made the wilderness sprout and bloom, and your sufferings made your labor fruitful a hundredfold; you became a shining torch over the world, O Holy Father Theodosius. Pray to Christ God that he may save our souls" (Troparion for the Feast).

MAR SABA

Outside the monastery gates I took out my little map and went over to where several men were standing. I pointed to the monastery of the great Mar Saba, the Sanctified, as he is called in the liturgy. ("Mar" is the Syriac word for "Saint.") They gave me some directions and I set out. I had planned to do a lot of walking that day, a pilgrimage of thanksgiving for all the desert fathers. It was not an extremely warm day, but it wasn't cool either. I began my walk into the desert.

Several years ago I had drawn up a "Litany of Hermits" that I used to say. I wished I had brought it along with me. However, I knew enough desert fathers to pray some of this litany as I made my way to Mar Saba:

Jesus, King of Hermits, have mercy of me.
Elias, pray for me.
Eliseus   "
John the Baptist
St. Paul
St. Anthony
St. Pachomius
St. Hilarion
St. Euthymius
Abba Moses
Abba Isaac
St. Mary of Egypt
St. Thais
St. Melania
St. Paula,
St. Juliana
St. John Climacus
St. Theodosius
St. Saba
St. Seraphim of Sarov

St. Theophane the Recluse
St. Bruno
St. Ephrem
St. Charbel

It was my first walk through a real desert, and I was going to visit the great Mar Saba. My heart was filled with gratitude for all these desert heroes and heroines who, by their courage and love, bequeathed to us such magnificient treasures of the spiritual life. One of the reasons we should be so grateful to the saints is that they showed us what human nature, joined to the Spirit of Christ, is capable of. Without them, our vision would be so small, so mediocre. We would tend to consider the Gospel "beautiful but way out of our reach." The saints reveal to us the possibilities of holiness, and give us hope in putting flesh on our visions of love.

As I was walking along I thought too of the thousands of miles walked by the desert fathers during their lifetimes. It is recorded that Anthony of Egypt (on whose feast I am now writing) could still walk twenty miles up to the day he died. He died at the age of one hundred and five. I prayed for a share in the spirit of all these great men and women.

Finally, I arrived at the top of a hill and came in full view of the monastery of Mar Saba. It was a thrilling sight for me. I sat down for a few moments and just took it all in. There was a sign at the entrance of the road: "Monastery of Mar Saba. Entrance to women forbidden. Please respect the sanctity of this holy place."

As I was to learn shortly, this road spreading before me towards the monastery was only a few months old . It had been built by the government for tourist purposes. The monks didn't really want it because it brought more visitors into their life. It seems Tourism is one of the new gods, and everything is sacrificed to it, even holy places such as this. I arose and began my descent.

On the road to the monastery a monk came walking towards me. My first Palestinian monk! I wonder if he speaks English ? Turns out he was an American from California ! He wasn't a professed monk, had only been here two years; he wasn't sure if he would stay. It was a very difficult life. He had been born and raised in the Catholic Church, but it was only here, in the East, that he discovered the sense of mystery for which his soul was longing.

He told me that I was arriving on a very special day, the feast of the return of Mar Saba's body from Italy. The Crusaders had carried it away in the twelfth century; Pope Paul VI had it returned in 1965. Saba's body is incorrupt.

He also told me what recent archeological findings were revealing. During Sabas' lifetime there were cells here for 15,000 monks. Archeologists say that the monks kept building out from the caves, so that the total effect would have resembled a six-story apartment building. Before we parted he said, "Be sure to ask if you can see the tomb of St. John Damascene. They don't show it to everybody."

Whenever I meet someone who has left the Catholic Church, I still believe I am his or her spiritual father. Indeed, the mind of the Church is that a priest is father to all the people in his area, whether actually Catholic or not. Much of modern Catholic practice has lost the sense of mystery and of the transcendent. This young man was a product of that loss – and he had come half-way around the world to quench his thirst for mystery.

I arrived at the monastery door, rang the bell, and a monk opened the door. He seemed relieved to see that I was alone, looking around to see if anyone else was there. His attitude raised hopes in me that I was in for a special treat. I was not disappointed.

As did the nun at St. Theodosius, this monk likewise escorted me immediately into the catholicon, the monastic church proper. And I had the same experience as before. You are hit with an avalanche of holiness and spiritual presences. There are icons everywhere, and, in this particular monastery, the worship of Christ had continued uninterrupted for 1,500 years. He then led me to venerate the incorrupt body of St. Saba the Sanctified.

I can't put into words the profound spiritual experience this venerating of the body of Saba was for me. I have a great love for the desert fathers and their unparalleled contribution to Christian life. Saba was a disciple of Euthymius the Great (377-473) who lived in a cave between Jerusalem and Jericho. I believe Euthymius had met the great St. Anthony of Egypt. (When I was in Thessalonica I bought an icon print of St. Anthony and St. Euthymius, side by side.) Euthymius touched Anthony, and Sabas touched Euthymius; now I am touching the body of Sabas. The kissing of his relics suddenly deepened my relationship with all the desert fathers. In some way they became living persons for me.

Saba was born in Cappadocia in 439, and

I can't put into words the profound spiritual experience this venerating of the body of St. Saba was for me. I have a great love for the desert fathers and their unparalleled contribution to Christian life.

entered monastic life while still a youth. Because of his maturity of mind Euthymius called him the "Young Old Man." When Euthymius died in 473, Saba spent five years in complete reclusion in the wilderness, and then established himself in a cave on the left bank of the river Cedron.

As part of my tour, my gracious monk-host took me outside to a porch overlooking this same Cedron stream. He pointed to a cave in the hill opposite, and said: "That's the cave where Saba lived. One day our Lady appeared to him and told him to build a church in this natural cave here on this side of the Cedron."

The original church I had visited was, in fact, a large cave. Celestus, the Patriarch of Jerusalem, had it transformed into a church which he consecrated. On the same occasion he ordained Saba to the priesthood and established him as Grand-Archimandrite over all the hermits in Palestine. (The title "archimandrite" was usually given to the head of a monastery. It means "shepherd of the sheep.") Saba died on December 5, 532, at the age of ninety-three.

I was then taken to a little chapel where the skulls of hundreds of monks were kept. Many of these had been martyred by the Persians in the 6th century. I prayed for the grace of courage in the face of opposition to the Gospel. It makes one realize that down through the centuries hundred of thousands of people have been killed for their faith; it is still happening. How small my crosses seemed as I looked at that stark pile of skulls.

Next, I was taken (without having requested it, so I knew our Lady was opening doors for me) to venerate the tomb of St. John Damascene

(d. 749). He is one of the great Fathers of the church. In patristic literature he is often called the "Last of the Fathers" because many of his writings were summaries of the Church's teaching up to his time. He spent many years as a monk of this monastery, and died here at an advanced age. In the West, Pope Leo XIII declared him a doctor of the universal Church.

My experience of venerating his tomb was similar to that of Saba. I had never in my life been this close to one of the Fathers of the Church. As I kissed his tomb they all came alive – Basil, and the Gregories, Chrysostom and Cyril – they all took on flesh and blood. I only had a few minutes at St. John's tomb, but it was enough; I had touched him. I only had a few minutes to wait on the presence, but I am forever linked with him and the Fathers in a new way.

I was served a delightful lunch of wine, bread, olives, fish, and fruit. I ate alone on the little balcony overlooking the many caves in the hills. I was allowed to stay for None and Vespers. It was to be the first of many prayer experiences with Orthodox monks. Presently there were only a dozen or so in this monastery, but I thought to myself, "If they've come through 1,500 years, it's hard to imagine what could possibly put an end to their life now." I prayed for their fervent continuation.

I will always be grateful to this monk. He was a true son of the hospitable Theodosius and Saba. The night before he had been up nine hours chanting the whole liturgy of the feast of Saba. He looked very tired, and yet he spared no time and effort to make my visit a fruitful one.

As I was about to leave I asked his blessing. He said he wasn't a priest and therefore couldn't give a blessing. We shook hands, and I slipped out of the old wooden door and returned to the desert.

There are still bandits in the area; we call them children. In the earlier part of the day all the bandits are kept in one place; we call it a school. But at this time of day, late afternoon, the territory is dangerous.

Some of the bandits are lovely. As I walked away from Mar Saba I saw two little shepherd girls run a very great distance to waylay me. It was a pleasure to be robbed by them, and I was generous. But one cannot always be generous, especially when you are attacked by a whole band.

As I continued on I watched a whole game of kick-ball mysteriously move from a field into the street where I had to pass. Sure enough, the game stopped at some secret signal and I was surrounded. In such a situation, if you give to one, you must give to all. It unfortunately got a little unpleasant, but I managed to escape. They were trying to find out what language I spoke, so I muttered some tongue that was incomprehensible even to myself. Walking can have some of these inconveniences, but the advantages, as far as I am concerned, are worth it. I arrived at the bus station and rode the rest of the way to Bethlehem.

RETURN TO THE CAVE
AND THE SHEPHERDS' FIELD

I learned from one of the Sisters that liturgies took place at the Cave early in the morning. So I rose and went to the shrine about 6 A.M. Sure enough, an Orthodox priest was preparing the gifts. Because of the presence of the Eastern rite at Madonna House, I was familiar with this very symbolic preparation.

When the first cut is made in the bread the priest says, "As a sheep he was led to the slaughter." At the second cut, "As a spotless lamb silent before its shearer, he opens not his mouth." And cutting into the symbol of the lamb, "The lamb of God who takes away the sins of the world is immolated for the life and salvation of the world."

As the priest was performing this rite I thought 1 would go up and ask him if I could receive Communion. I told him I was a Roman Catholic priest. He thought for a moment and then said, rather gruffly, "No!" I wasn't too surprised – a bit disappointed, but it was okay. I went to the back of the Cave since I was going to stay for the Liturgy. I began praying for the priest's peace, that our little exchange wouldn't dampen his spirit before the liturgy.

All of a sudden the priest's assistant came over and motioned me to go and see the priest again. The priest said, "Where are you from ?" I said, "Canada." He said, "You may stay." I did stay, and was given Holy Communion as well. This experience was the first of many where the pain of Christian unity entered my heart in a new way. It was that morning when I first began thinking of doing more penance for the unity of Christians, especially between east and west.

I took a walk around the town of Bethlehem that morning. I was given a private tour of an ancient Syrian Orthodox church by an affable old deacon who was on duty. I reverenced an Aramaic Old Testament which was 1,500 years old, and a New Testament 400 years old. He handed me a prayer card on which the Our Father was written in Aramaic. I asked him to recite it for me, and he did. It was the first time I heard the Lord's Prayer in sounds similar to how Jesus first spoke it. He also had in his hand what seemed to be prayer beads. I said, "Oh, your prayer beads ?" "No," he said. "I'm an old man. These are not for praying but for playing."

I went by but to see the church of Mar Elias. A young Greek monk let me in. Again, behind the drab exterior of the building was a magnificent church filled with beautiful icons. There was an ancient icon of Eliseus beseeching Elias for a share in his spirit. This became a theme for me in so many places – asking for a share in the spirit of the great saints of the shrines. Here, I asked for a share in the spirit of Elias – not a double portion (!) but a share, according to my capacity.

Then I went back to the Basilica to visit the cave where St. Jerome wrote his commentaries and translated the bible into Latin.

I just sat there. Initially the spiritual significance of these places immobilized me. This is where a translation of the bible was made which influenced, beyond calculation, the mind of the Western Church for 1,500 years. It was another first contact with the great spiritual tradition of the Church, this time with a towering figure in the field of the transmission of the scripture.

I breathed a prayer of gratitude for the thousands and thousands of people down through the centuries who have copied and handed on to us the sacred texts. With printing so commonplace today we forget that for most of the Christian tradition the bible had to be copied by hand, consuming untold hours and efforts. I often imagine our brothers and sisters copying, by the dim light of candles, this holiest of books which we now pop into a bookstore and buy in five minutes.

While sitting in Jerome's cave my thought also turned to his feminine companions, Eustochium and Paula. They and their followers were very close to Jerome. The women had several monasteries in the area, but they also must have spent quite a bit of time with Jerome, tending to his needs, profiting from his direction and learning, "domesticating" his somewhat irascible character.

Their relationship was one of the earliest and closest Christian associations of men and women united in the spiritual quest. I prayed to Jerome and Paula and Marcella to intercede for us here at Madonna House. We also have been called to strive together as men and women in a special kind of Christian community.

Next, I walked to the Shepherds' Field. The church there was built by the Canadian people, so I sent Prime Minister Trudeau a postcard, telling him how much I appreciated the chapel, and that I prayed here for the Canadian people.

As I walked around the open fields I was moved to pray for a deepening of the sense of wonder. The expanse of sky out here was immense. The angels are always praising God in decibals too loud for us to hear. But here, in these fields, at least for one night in the history of the world, the sound barrier was removed. Some poor shepherds were admitted to the heavenly symphony which is always being performed. They heard and they believed. May we also be able to hear the angelic choirs, at least with the ears of faith.

Tour guides say some peculiar things. I copied this one down word for word as I was sitting in the cave where tradition says the shepherds were lodged that holy night. The guide said: "Catholics give a great deal of importance to places. We Protestants are closer to the Jews who worship the idea. The Greek Orthodox go to the other extreme and worship places." I'm sure he wasn't aware that a Roman Catholic priest was there listening.

An impish urge took hold of me, but I resisted. I felt like standing up and saying, "Well, if places are not really important to you, why have you come half-way around the world to be here in this little cave in the hill?" Places are important to Christians because we believe God really became a Man. Our religion is not an idea. (And, by the way, neither is it for the Jews. There are places sacred to the Jews all over Palestine.) The Christian faith is all about God entering our history, actually inserting himself in our flesh, our towns, our hillsides. Places are important because our incarnate God really touched them.

Shortly afterwards a Black Pentecostal group came in. It was a totally different scene. They were singing and praising God with all their might. Several came over where I was sitting and wished me the peace of Christ. At these shrines you witness devotional practices of different Christian denominations. It is an education in the diversity of christian culture and attitudes.

You will remember that I had given away my little New Testament. Well, as I was walking back to Bethlehem I saw a sign which read: "Bethlehem Bible College." I went in and asked if they had any pocket New Testaments for sale. A man graciously went into a room and came out with just what I wanted. He wouldn't take any money for it. "Cast your bread on the waters and it will return to you."

Before I left a young man briefly engaged me in conversation. He was interested to learn that I was a Roman Catholic priest. He himself was born in the Greek Orthodox Church, "but now I have been saved from all those practices," he said. I prayed that some day, as his Christian soul matured, he would come to understand "those practices."

I arrived back in Bethlehem about 4:30 in the afternoon and decided to spend more time in the holy Cave. I could never get enough. I went in and sat in prayer for about a half-hour or so. Only myself and a Franciscan priest were present. I decided to approach the sacred spot on the floor marked with the fourteen-point gold star, one for each of the generations of Christ's ancestry. (One of the guides said it was for the fourteen stations of the Cross!) I prostrated full length on the floor with my head on the star. After a few moments the priest left and for fifteen more minutes I was all alone in the Cave, prostrate on the spot where God came forth from Mary.

I think that, after the Holy Sepulchre, that

After a few moments the priest left and for fifteen more minutes I was all alone in the Cave of Bethlehem, prostrate on the spot where God came forth from Mary.

period of fifteen minutes was the high-point of my pilgrimage. In the tomb he returned to life; here he first came forth into our world. There were no thoughts. I was just flooded with wonder and praise and thanksgiving for the Incarnation. God the Word made flesh among us.

No, I was not worshipping this spot, this place, this cave. But our God, by touching this place, by taking on my flesh, by having a Mother, brought his Reality into our human tent in a way no mere idea or doctrine could ever accomplish. This is why when anyone professes belief in this God who became a man, a whole new dimension of reality is opened up for that person. God then becomes as close to that person as he possibly can. This is the presence of the Holy Spirit.

It was time to lock up. I was asked by the caretaker to leave. Thank you, Lord, for reserving the Cave for me for these precious moments. O Bethlehem ! Land of Jesus and Mary and Joseph ! City of David ! Home of Saba and Theodosius and Jerome and Paula and John Damascene, how blessed you are ! Truly you are by no means least among the towns of Juda. I love you, Bethlehem, House of Bread which housed the Bread of Life! I kiss your ground and your soil and your fields.

My last day in Bethlehem arrived. There was to be a solemn high Latin Mass at the Manger. (The Greek Orthodox care for the site of the Birth of Christ, and the Latins care for the Manger which is just a few feet away.)

The Mass was beautifully done. One of the graces I received during the celebration was a profound gratitude for being Roman Catholic. Maybe it was the atmosphere, maybe it was the sense of belonging and of being welcomed, but whatever it was I experienced a marked freshness and vitality about the liturgy that morning. It was all in Latin, and so you had the sense of belonging to the ancient Church for sure !

On the other hand, there were some young Italian Sisters there who sang light and melodious contemporary songs in their own language. I will always hear those lovely songs in the Cave, because they sang to me that this faith is ancient but every new. It will never die. Truly the liturgy was a combination of the old and the new, blended in a marvelous way. I was happy and proud and thankful for being a member of this Church which continually brings out of her storehouse "things old and new."

I knew this would be my last visit to the Cave, perhaps for the rest of my life. There was no sadness, no regret. I was always aware that, in some real way, I didn't *need* places. The deepest truth is that wherever I am I can enter ever more deeply into the beauty of Bethlehem.. The mystery of the Presence is everywhere now because "Christ is in you, your hope of glory." The saints who had never been to these holy places were present to Christ in their hearts. (Gregory of Nyssa is certainly right here !) In this way they imbibed the riches of each of the aspects of the total mystery of Christ. And I could too; with God's help, I will.

I remained praying for about an hour and a half, and then the caretaker came through and said, "Ten more minutes! Ten more minutes!" Altogether during these few days I had spent five or six hours in the Cave. What a gift !

Finally, I rose from my knees and went to kiss the Star for the last time. As I walked out of the Church I didn't have the feeling that I was walking away from the Star. The Star is everywhere now. Christmas means that (in the words of W.H.Auden) "Everything is a You, and nothing is an it." The whole universe is personal now because Heaven has wedded earth; God has become one of us.

It was a great grace to have kissed the place of Christ's birth; it will be even more of a grace to kiss him in every person I meet and in every aspect of creation.

CHAPTER SIX

Jericho, Bethany, Farewell to Jerusalem

Around 10 A.M. I took a sherut back to Jerusalem. I returned to Ecce Homo and packaged some gifts to mail to Canada. By the way, this is easier than carrying your gifts around with you from place to place. They arrived in Canada safe and sound. It's a little expensive, but well worth the cost.

I spent the rest of the day and evening unpacking – but not my luggage. "Unpacking" is one of my favorite expressions for one of life's most essential functions.

In a book by Chesterton, *The Well and the Shadows*, in a chapter entitled "The Case for Hermits," he writes:

> The reason why even the normal human being should be half a hermit is that it is the only way in which his mind can have half a holiday. It bears the most resemblance to the unpacking of luggage.... Many of us live in a luggage van, or wander about the world with luggage we never unpack at all. For the best things that happen to us are those we get out of what has already happened.

On the one hand there are the experiences of life, and on the other hand the unpacking, the digesting, the assimilation of these experiences. We speak of "superficial experiences." In one real sense, all experiences are superficial if we do not assimilate them into the deeper core of the personality, or reject them from the core.

For too many people life is a jumble of experiences which have never been assimilated. Their internal life is like a baggage compartment of unpacked experiences. Much confusion about "who we are" come from our failure to unpack. Our internal experience has not yet been sorted out. Of all the things that have happened to us, we literally do not know which we want to incorporate into our deeper being, and which we do not. It is no wonder we don't know who we are.

No doubt, after one returns from a pilgrimage, many hours are spent in the telling and the reminiscing. But there should be time for this even on the pilgrimage itself. It is so easy to be continually on the go, caught up in planning, traveling, seeing, packing and unpacking (luggage) that one spends no time at all assimilating precious experiences after they happen. I allowed myself time to do this on my pilgrimage.

The poet Wallace Stevens put it this way: "I don't know which to prefer... the blackbird whistling, or just after." Over and over again I found the quiet time spent in my room "just after" visiting the holy places as enriching and precious as the actual events. Pilgrims need time for this kind of savoring of Presences.

JERICHO

The next day, Saturday, October 29, I took a sherut to Jericho. I wanted to visit the Monastery of the Temptation and walk around the desert area where Jesus fasted and was tempted by the devil. Arriving in Jericho I walked the several miles out of town and up the mountain to the monastery. Because of my love for the desert the mystery of Christ in the wilderness has a very special significance for me.

In scripture, the desert is the place where God often reveals himself in a comforting, caring way. "Desert" in the scriptures often draws our minds to the terrible theophanies on Sinai, the punishments meted out to the rebels in the desert, and the temptations of Christ by the devil. But if you read the whole of scripture you will note that most of the time the desert is the place of comfort and consolation . I cite just one story of many – Hagar, in Genesis 16.

Hagar, Abraham's concubine, had been thrown out into the desert through the jealousy of Sarai. "The Lord's messenger found her by a spring in the wilderness." The Lord tells her to go back, suffer Sarai's abuse, and he will make of her descendants a great people. This was a great consolation indeed. Not only that, but the vision of the Lord is not terrifying: "To the Lord who spoke to her she gave a name, saying, 'You are the God of Vision'; she meant, 'Have I seen God and remained alive after my vision?' " In Hebrew the place was called Beer-lahai-roi which means "the well of living sight, the well where one can see God and yet live."

Elias is comforted in the wilderness. And even Moses ' burning bush experience is awesome – holy – but not terrifying. More often than not, God reveals himself as a God of consolation in the desert.

Jesus goes into the desert mostly to pray, to commune with his Father. He was to preach to the poeple that when they wished to pray, "go into your secret chambers, close the door, and pray to your Father in secret." Jesus went off to pray alone to his Father all his life. He loved to do this. so, at the beginning of his public mission, he goes off into the wilderness to commune intimately with his Father. He goes also to confront satan; but the scriptures say that he first had forty days of deep prayer, and then he was tempted.

Here I was, at the site where Jesus was driven by the Spirit into the wilderness to conquer the first enemy blocking our return to paradise. Here, in this desert, Jesus won for us all our battles against Satan. Satan was definitively defeated here. He only continues to have power because people do not believe he has been defeated. Satan knows he has been defeated. He keeps people from believing in Christ lest his defeat be revealed. His power is built, as always, on lies. I was walking now on the field of one of the greatest victories of all times.

I arrived at the door of the monastery and rang the bell. This Monastery of the Temptation was built by St. Helena in the 4th century. The door was opened, not by a monk but by a Muslim caretaker who had been working here for twenty years. I learned that only five monks were here at the present time; during my visit I never saw one. I was led again into a beautiful church filled with icons. Some of them were 600 years old. After reverencing them I was led up a stone staircase and shown a rock formation surrounded by vigil lights and icons. I was told that this was the traditional spot of the temptation of Christ. I asked if I could pray here for a few minutes, and he said yes.

I prayed especially for an absolute belief in Christ's victory over evil spirits, for discernment

This Monastery of the Temptation was built by St. Helena in the 4th century. I prayed that everyone would believe that what Christ did here in the desert had absolute and unquestionable finality. Satan has been conquered; his power is broken forever. He knows it, but do we?

to know when they are tempting me and others, and for courage in combating them should people come to me seeking the power of Christ in my priesthood. I have been involved in some actual deliverances in my priestly ministry. During those experiences I have had powerful confirmations of the victory of Christ.

Oh, I prayed that everyone would believe that what Christ did here in the desert had absolute and unquestionable finality. Satan *has been* conquered; his power is broken forever. *He* knows it, but do we ? Unfortunately, we do not. and because of our lack of faith in Christ's victory, we continue to give Satan power that has been taken away from him. In Christ's victory we have already conquered. May we believe more firmly that his victory is completely in us, especially in our combat with evil spirits.

When the caretaker returned he told me that the monastery is practically deserted. Young men come, but the life is too hard for them. He said a hermit presently lives in one of the caves near the monastery. I knew it would be impossible, but I asked if I might visit him. He said it was impossible ! I thanked him and left.

As I walked down the mountain I found a little cave of my own where I sat and prayed for a half-hour. Here, in this silence, in this desert place, was the confrontation between Christ and Satan. "O Christ of the wilderness, may your victory have its full sway in me. Help me, in your name, to meet and conquer the evil in me and around me. I believe in your total victory. Help my unbelief."

From my little cave near the top of the mountain I looked out upon a vast panorama—"all the kingdoms of the world" Just opposite from where I was I could see other caves in the hillsides. Is that where the hermit was? Again, I asked for a share in the spirit of the desert fathers, those giants who lived here in the desert on God alone. In my own poustinik life, how far I am from this absoluteness! Here there is nothing but God. How my spirit longs to have nothing but God.

Christ's fasting came to mind, forty days in the desert without food. I tried to enter into this mystery, praying for the grace of true penance. He spent weeks out here, eating nothing at all. What power was in him! No wonder the devils were afraid he would despoil their kingdom. I recalled what the devil had said to St. John Vianney one day: "If there were six people like you, my kingdom could not stand." We possess an immense spiritual weapon in fasting; how few of us have the courage to use it.

What also came over me as I was sitting in this little cave was a deep sense of the dignity of the human person. Our spirit is meant to rule supremely over every other aspect of our being. The spirit can breathe here in the wilderness. How we allow this great spiritual being that each of us is to be dragged down by idols and appetites of all kinds. We were meant to rule over all creation, and we allow all of creation to rule over us. "O Christ, give me a greater portion of your Spirit so that I might be restored into your true image and likeness, and reflect the great dignity of the human person."

I continued my walk down the mountain

and back to Jericho, where I grabbed a taxi to Jerusalem.

This was to be my last visit in the City of David. Early in the evening I once again climed the Mount of Olives. I met my Arab tourist-agent friend and went to his home for a chat and a cup of coffee. Then I returned to my strolling and praying.

I received a tangible grace that evening. My thoughts turned again to the loneliness of Christ. Catherine, in one of her writings, has a poignant phrase about this aspect of the Lord: "Nobody knew who he was, inside of himself."

As I was pondering his immense aloneness he spoke a word to me of how I might console him. He said that every act of penance I perform would console him in his loneliness. I have always believed this; this evening he confirmed the truth of it in my heart. I promised him something that evening, and put a symbol of this promise in one of the trees on the Mount. The wind has probably blown it away by now, but for me it will always be there. Whenever I am tempted to go back on my promise, I see the symbol I placed in the tree that evening.

He also spoke a word to me about meditating on his Passion: I am weak in penance and bearing the cross because I no longer meditate very much on his pain and wounds. We emphasize the resurrection so much these days that we have forgotten about the Passion. In *The Way of a Pilgrim,* every time one of the pilgrim's friends was tempted to drink, he would read a passage from the scriptures. This would fortify him against alcohol.

The Lord said to me that the remembrance of his Passion could become just such a strength for me. He said that if each time I was tempted to go back on my promise of penance, if I would open the scriptures and read a section on his Passion, that this would fortify me in my resolve.

Sunday morning I spent two hours at liturgies in the Holy Sepulchre. At a Spanish Mass on Mt. Calvary I noticed the people touching and kissing everything, just like the Byzantines! Then I went to the Cenàcle for the last time.

My meditation that morning turned to the holy community that used to meet here. Imagine celebrating Eucharist with our Lady, the Apostles, Mary Magdalene, Mary and Cleophas, Lazarus, Martha and Mary--all in one room! Oh the depth of their faith and love! Imagine them talking about Jesus' life, about his resurrection appearances, about what he said to them on various occasions. And the Spirit was moving powerfully in them to understand "everything that I have told you." Has there ever been, since those Eucharists in this Upper Room, an agape such as were celebrated here!

I prayed especially for our little church of Madonna House, that we too would continue to be a strong faith community, joyful in our belief in the Resurrection, and courageous in bearing whatever trials the Lord might send our way.

For several days I had been trying, unsuccessfully, to contact Fr. Raphael at Emmaus. On my way to catch the bus for Bethany that morning a car stopped to let somebody out. It was Fr. Raphael! This was truly a gift from the Lord. The very next day I was planning to leave for Galilee, and I was hoping he could make some arrangement for me. I was not disappointed. Right there on the street he wrote out for me a letter of introduction to his Franciscan brothers at the Church of the Primacy of Peter in Tabgha. Then I hopped on a bus for Bethany.

BETHANY

I arrived around noon. The church was closed. Lazarus' tomb is always open so I went there first. It must be 25 or 30 feet down into the ground. I stepped into the tomb proper, lighted only by a bulb on a cord. A young couple was sitting there, silently. I sat down also. In a minute or two they went back up and I was left there alone. I started to take out my New Testament to read about the raising of Lazarus, when the light went out! I panicked for a moment. "Maybe they are locking the door!" I called out, but not too loudly, for then I remembered the sign outside saying that the tomb was open all afternoon. I guessed, rightly, that they were just turning out the light. So I didn't call out any more.

So here I was in Lazarus' tomb, in absolute darkness, except for a faint shaft of light coming down the stairs. It only took me a moment to realize that this was somehow a special gift from the Lord, to be sitting here in darkness in the tomb of Lazarus. And it *was* a gift. The Lord drew me into a very profound meditation about death.

Here is where Lazarus lay for several days, perhaps right where I'm sitting, wrapped in embalming clothes. The air presently was a bit heavy, but I'm sure nothing like those days when, as Martha said, "surely there is a stench." Here he lay – one day, two days, three days. Where was he ? Where was his soul ? Then, on the fourth day, a voice came strong, powerful, and irresistible booming down these stairs into this darkness: "Lazarus, come forth !" And this body, this corpse, this inert matter which had been lying here for four days, began to stir.

There was a squirming, an expanding of the cloth bands, and then, with slow but determined efforts, the legs slowly swing down from the stone slab onto the ground. The voice keeps commanding in the darkness – "Come forth! Come forth! Come forth!" It is the Word of the Word, the Word through whom everything was made, the Word who creates by speaking. Nothing can resist his commands. "Come! Come! Come!"

And this being – Lazarus by name – which is once again fully human, obeys the Word, and slowly climbs up, up towards the thin ray of light at the entrance. He still cannot see; he sees by hearing. The stone has been rolled away, the light of day is pouring in, but he only sees the Word. He steps out into the light and his friends gently, and as if in a daze unbind him and let him go free.

Such it will be for me. I will be buried in the earth, in a dark coffin. I will be in my priestly clothes. Then one day I will hear, from the lips of the risen Lord, what Lazarus heard that day: "Robert, my priest, come forth!" And from wherever the separate parts have been, this all – powerful Word, Jesus, will draw them together. And I will rise from sleep and go to him.

I sat in that tomb, in the dark, for an hour. I kept hearing, "Robert, come forth! Robert, come forth!" I knew that if I were faithful to Christ for just a little bit longer, I would certainly one day hear those words. Then, nothing in the whole universe would ever again be able to prevent me from coming to Jesus. That voice, that Word, "Come !" would draw me through darkness, through the realms of Satan, through sin and death, and pull me as a magnet into Christ's arms. That Sunday morning in Lazarus' tomb I received a solid assurance that I too would rise from the dead.

We laugh at the practice of the ancient monks who consciously tried to keep the thought of death ever in mind: "As bread is the most necessary food, so the memory of death among other virtues; it is impossible for a hungry man not to recall bread; likewise for the man striving to be saved, it is impossible not to recall death."

We write this off as morbid and anti-life. We are the blind ones. Ernst Becker in his *The Denial of Death* showed how this denial of death is the cause in us of much of what we label "original sin." We live with emergency brakes on. We are moving towards death with the speed of light, but we make believe we will never arrive

I sat in that tomb, in the dark, for an hour. I kept hearing "Robert, come forth!" I knew that if I were faithful to Christ for just a little bit longer...

there. We have both feet on the brakes.

Those people who have had positive "life after life" experiences witness in their consciousness to a new burst of freedom and creativity. They are not afraid now of death, so neither are they afraid of life. The two go together somehow. The fear of death (which Jesus has freed us from, Heb. 2:15) also prevents us from living. The ancient monks knew this. Let us admit we are afraid of death, and that's why we don't think about it. The monks were not afraid to think about it, and that's one reason why they were most alive.

After an hour I decided to leave. There was a bit of light. I slowly made my way up the stairs and out into the sunlight. As I emerged I heard in my imagination, "Unbind him and let him go free." A young woman, the caretaker of the tomb, saw me and said with a gasp, "You were down there ! I didn't know!" I just smiled. For some reason I was very hungry. I felt as if I had just gone on some immense journey and back. I went and had lunch.

FAREWELL TO JERUSALEM

I returned to Jerusalem and visited once again the churches of the Flagellation and Gethsemane. I also spent two more hours on my beloved Mount of Olives. When I pray now I often join my prayer to Christ who is somehow still spending whole nights there "in prayer to God."

When I returned to Ecce Homo I was invited by Sr. Donna to have supper with the Sisters and spend my last evening with them. It was a gracious offer and a delightful way to end my stay in Jerusalem. The Sisters of Sion have dedicated their lives to a special mission: that the people of Israel might one day come into the fullness of their inheritance -- Christ. Their founder was a Jewish rabbi who was converted to Christ in Rome through an apparition of our Lady. The Sisters were always very helpful in assisting me and in making my stay fruitful. May God bless their work!

I rose early on my last day in Jerusalem and went, with my packed luggage, to a Latin high Mass at 6:30 A.M. in the Holy Sepulchre. On this, my last visit to Calvary, I offered myself in some new way as a victim in union with Christ. By our baptism we are all sharers in his victimhood, but perhaps priests in a special way are drawn into this mystery. There were no specific promises or resolutions; we usually don't keep them anyhow. I simply made a deeper gift of myself in union with Christ on the Cross who is our Priest, and our Victim. I prostrated one final time before the Cross of my salvation, and then I departed for Galilee.

CHAPTER SEVEN

GALILEE: TABGHA, NAZARETH, TABOR, TABGHA

Each place in the Holy land had its special grace and spiritual atmosphere for me. Jerusalem was noisy and often tense. It is the focal point for Christian, Jewish, and Muslim sensitivities, with these people rubbing, jostling, and clashing with one another on a daily basis. You feel it all the time. Yet, you still sense it is the holiest city in the world.

Bethlehem, though not far from Jerusalem, breathes a different atmosphere. Perhaps it's the calming effect a baby has anywhere. People can be tense and edgy in a room together. When a baby is brought in, everyone smiles and relaxes. In Bethlehem everyone is looking at the Child.

At Tabgha, my next stop, I experienced in a prolonged, constant fashion, the presence of the risen Christ. He exploded upon me in the tomb. Here he seemed to walk with me at every moment. Strange, but Tabgha was the only place I felt a little sad in leaving.

After leaving Jerusalem I took a bus to Tiberias on the Sea of Galilee. The first sight of this beautiful sea already imparts a calming, restful effect after the starkness of the southern deserts. I took a taxi the short distance to Tabgha. We passed some ruins on the right and the driver said, "Magdala." Immediately that magnificent person, Mary, came to mind.

It has been said that the gospels are not so much complete accounts of the life of Christ as stage directions for a drama. It's true in a way.

We only have a few lines about a Man's whole life. What happened in between ? As regards Mary Magdalen, for example. She loved him so much, and she was the first person reported in the Gospel to see the risen Lord. As Jesus was making his long journey back to us he thought to himself, "Now whom shall I visit first ?" Our hearts tell us he went to see his Mother. But then he appeared to Mary Magdalene as one of the first he desired to see. I believe that: he **wanted** to see her. He must have loved her very much.

Surely she was not always just following him around at a distance in a crowd of women. They must have often talked together, walked together. What did they talk about ? People called to celibacy -- but everyone called to purity – struggle with friendships and relationships with members of the opposite sex. Jesus' relationship to Mary is the mystery we need to enter into. He loved her completely and purely and intensely. "Lord, teach us how to be friends with each other. And Mary, obtain for us the grace to fall in love with Jesus as you did."

Tabgha is the name given to the site of three gospel occurrences – the Multiplication of the Loaves and Fishes, the resurrection appearance along the shore of the lake (The primacy of Peter), and the Sermon on the Mount. "Tabgha" is an arabic abbreviation of an old Greek name for "Seven Springs," because of the abundance of springs which characterize the area.

Recent archeology confirms the presence of a Jewish-Christian community in nearby Capharnaum in the early centuries. It is from this community that pilgrims gathered the living tradition of these three holy places. The sanctuary of the Primacy of Peter is taken care of by the Franciscan Fathers; the Basilica of the Multiplication of the Loaves by the German Benedictines. Guided by Fr. Raphael's directions, and with his letter of introduction in hand, I rang the bell of the gate leading to that wonderful appearance of Jesus on the shore.

I was graciously let in by Brother Michel. As the door to the dusty road closed behind me I knew immediately that I was in another world. The breeze from the sea hit my face; at the same time the presence of the risen Christ hit my soul. Both were to last my entire stay.

The resurrection appearance commemorated here is, of course, from John's Gospel, Chapter 21: "Later on, Jesus showed himself again to the disciples. It was by the Sea of Tiberias, and it happened like this." There follows the account of the miraculous catch of fish, Jesus cooking breakfast for them at a charcoal fire, and Jesus' conversation with Peter, "Do you love me?"

After getting settled in my room I went to the shore of the Lake. It was the first time I was able to touch the Lake, so I dipped my hand in and blessed myself. Jesus had walked on it, calmed it, perhaps even swam in it. It's still holy and always will be. I stood there on the shore. Even though it was afternoon I let the whole astounding episode of the Gospel wash over me like the waves that were now washing over the shore. I don't know exactly why the Lord gave me this grace, but it was at this site, for the duration of my stay, where the reality of the kingdom, the new creation, came alive for me. This site became for me one of the most perfect

Tabgha is the name given to the site of three Gospel occurrences—the Primacy of Peter, the Multiplication of the Loaves and Fishes, and the Sermon on the Mount.

images of human existence, which has now been permanently transformed by the presence of the risen Christ.

Here was a miraculous catch of fish. Here the apostles recognized the risen Lord. Here the New Adam peacefully walked up and down the shore in the morning hours. Here was the reunion of Jesus with his friends, sitting with them around a charcoal fire as the sun rose over the lake. Is not this the return to paradise ? Adam and Eve are no longer hiding from God. In the person of the apostles they are once again communing with God in the coolness of the new creation. As the hymn says, "God and man at table have sat down."

Between the church and the shore is a rock formation resembling stone stairs. "It was light by now and there stood Jesus on the shore." If someone wanted to call out to fishermen on the sea, this rock formation would be the obvious place to stand. At the beginning of the fifth century the famous pilgrim nun Etheria wrote about "some stone steps on which our Lord stood." I sat down on those steps and meditated and prayed for about an hour. I was often to return here in the course of the next few days.

Here Jesus stood in his resurrected glory. There must have been a divine playfulness in him that morning to have called out to his friends, "Hey, lads, have you caught anything ?" What a human/divine joy for him to surprise them like this, and all the while planning to make breakfast for them ! What a Saviour we have !

Then I went into the little church of the Primacy of Peter. Like Peter it is solid rock, with strong reds and blues in the stain-glassed windows. It shouts permanency and stability. Right in the center of the church was the rock upon which the Lord built the charcoal fire. The altar is situated just behind this rock so that when you are celebrating the Eucharist you gaze directly over it.

On two mornings I celebrated Mass here alone—just me, Christ, and the angels. It's hard to put into words the specific grace that came to me through those morning celebrations. It had something to do with the accessibility, the approachableness, of God. God became Man so that we might come close to him, not be afraid of him. The Baby in the crib is God of God, and Lord of Lords; yet, we can hold him in our arms. This is the time of mercy and forgiveness and love.

Although there are many non-threatening theophanies in the Old Testament, we, and the sacred writers as well, often recall the terrifying ones:

> You have not drawn near to an untouchable mountain, and a blazing fire, nor glooming darkness and storm and trumpet blast, nor a voice speaking words such that those who heard begged that they be not addressed to them, for they could not bear to hear the command: 'If even an animal touches the mountain, it must be stoned to death.' Indeed, so fearful was the spectacle that Moses said, 'I am terrified and trembling.' Now, you have drawn near... to Jesus, the mediator of a new covenant (Heb. 12:18-24).

This passage sums up best the grace I received. I saw Jesus puttering around that charcoal fire, cooking the fish, making sure the apostles, after fishing on the lake all night, were comfortable, and that they had what they needed. Jesus has done everything possible to make himself approachable—even to the making of our breakfast.

This grace continued to speak to me the next day when I walked up the Mount of the Beatitudes which rises directly from Tabgha. That morning I witnessed five different Masses going on, in five different places, in five different languages. I thought to myself: "I'm so glad I belong to the Roman rite which allows such simple Eucharists to take place."

I have been exposed to many Eastern rite liturgies which have been prayerfully celebrated; they have a splendor and magnificence all their own. But I thought of Emmaus; I thought of breakfast on the charcoal rock. It seems that Jesus himself opted for simplicity, for ordinariness, for accessibility. Here, on the Mount of Beatitudes, these pilgrims from all over the world were having breakfast with the risen Lord. The songs, the ritual, the vestments perhaps had much to be desired, but the essence was here: people feasting with the risen Lord.

There was a sadness that morning also. These people really had come from the north and south, east and west, and were taking their places at the feast in the kingdom of God, while many of the children of the promise were not at table. I experienced a constant sadness in the Holy Land, realizing that most of the people who lived there did not believe in Christ.

On the same day I climbed the Mount of Beatitudes I also walked to Capharnaum. On my way a convoy of tanks went by, throwing up quite a bit of dust. I reflected that the Lord must often have been walking along the roads when the Roman Legions went by: the symbols of worldly power passing the "powerless" Messiah in a cloud of dust.

I thought of all the discussions going on today about Jesus as a "revolutionary," and how the Gospel is being turned into another political theory. Jesus saw Roman power all his life; he knew he was living in an occupied country; he knew that there were various revolutionary factions at work to overthrow the Romans. And yet *never once* does he even hint that he is planning to move against these political powers. In all his speeches his adversaries could not find anything approaching political activity.

Don't we understand that Jesus' kingdom really is not of this world ? It wouldn't have mattered to him whether he said, instead of "Caesar," "Shah" or "King" or "Caliph." They're all the same for Jesus -- kingdoms of this world. He is not first of all preaching *against* any of the structures of the world. For him they're *all* infested with sin. What he has come to do is reveal an alternative way of living and loving -- the kingdom of God. It's totally opposite to all the worldly kingdoms, and cannot be achieved by over-throwing the latter. These are all born of the earth and are earthly; his kingdom is born of the Spirit and is heavenly. Jesus calls us to live in a new kingdom. If that kingdom spreads, all the others will eventually fall.

As the horses kicked dust in the Lord's face along the roads, he knew where real power lay.

His revolution was directed at the heart. His plan was to heal sin, and plant in the heart the seeds of a new way, the way of the beatitudes, the way of the kingdom of love. In Capharnaum he forgave a man's sins and restored him to health. This was the real revolution. All others which are built on sin and ignorance and the principles of the world simply prolong the disease. The kingdom of God is the only way to a new world.

I continued walking to Capharnaum. There are only ruins now. But as you walk around, if you listen closely, you can hear, hovering over the ruins, the discussions Jesus had with Peter about the temple tax (Matt. 17:24), and with the Centurion about his sick servant (8:5). If you are really quiet you can enter Peter's house (the ruins of which are still there) and see the Lord heal his mother-in-law, hear the commotion as all the people are freed from evil spirits (16). (I read once that no sound ever dies; it continues on somewhere in the universe. If that's true, then I believe the words of Jesus have a special "staying power." They are still in Capharnaum. I'm sure I heard them!)

I took the boat ride from Capharnaum to Tiberias and couldn't resist having a St. Peter's fish at a sea-side restaurant. (I wonder what it was called before St. Peter?)

On my first day at Tabgha I had stopped briefly at the church of the Multiplication of the Loaves. On this, my second day, I returned for a longer visit and prayer.

From archeological findings we know there was a church on this site in the fourth century; and a Byzantine church was built here in the fifth century. This latter was destroyed by the

Persians in the seventh century. However, many mosaics from the Byzantine church are still visible on the floor, especially one beautiful mosaic of the loaves and fishes right in front of the main altar. Seeing that 5th century mosaic makes your heart jump. I experienced a closeness with those brothers and sisters who worshipped on this site fifteen-hundred years ago. I arranged to celebrate the Eucharist here the following day.

There is a small chapel for private prayer where the Blessed Sacrament is reserved. Every time I went in the same elderly woman was there, praying. She was a Palestinian. At first I rather resented that I could never be alone in here, but soon she became a living symbol of all those sisters and brothers (perhaps her ancestors) who worshipped Christ here down through the centuries.

The grace I received in this shrine was trusting more in Providence. With Jesus we possess all the Father's care. On that special day so long ago, they had five loaves and two fish, plus *Jesus*! As our material, psychological, emotional goods dwindle, or seem to, what should increase is our awareness of our true wealth -- Jesus. He should be sufficient for us.

I have a practice of rising during the night for a prayer vigil. I continued this on my pilgrimage. If you've never tried it, please do. Night time is a very special period of prayer. There's something about the silence and dead of night which releases your soul, enabling it to soar into heights and depths that for some reason are not accessible during the day. Jesus often spent nights in prayer. Try it sometime.

On my third day at Tabgha I rose around midnight and went outside. It was warm, with a rather pronounced wind blowing. The sky was filled with a million stars. I walked down to the shore of the lake and sat on the steps where Jesus stood...

The Lord taught me some profound truths that night.

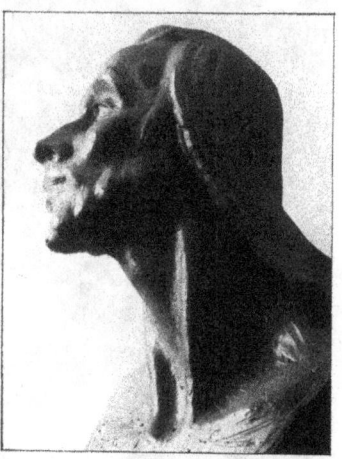

On my third day at Tabgha I rose around midnight and went outside. It was warm, with a rather pronounced wind blowing. The sky was filled with millions of stars. I walked down to the shore of the lake and sat on the steps where Jesus stood. The experience of the "return to paradise" which I mentioned earlier was intensified. The Lord taught me some profound truths that night.

We have such a minimal understanding of why Jesus came. For all practical purposes we allow the reality of "original sin" to dominate our efforts and awareness more than the grace of the Holy Spirit in us. Jesus did not come *simply* to help us control our anger. He did not come *simply* to forgive our sins. He did not come *simply* to help us get through another day without killing each other. *He came to restore us to paradise.* "Where sin abounded, grace did more abound." This means that, whatever original sin is, however it has affected our being, it is not deeper or more powerful than the original image of God in us, not deeper or more powerful than the presence of Christ and Holy Spirit in us.

It is important, the images we use of our beings tainted by original sin. What images should we use ? A diamond that has been dropped in the mud. The stem of a rose, bent but not broken, preventing the full flow of life. Water in a lake which has been polluted – but not beyond repair. I've chosen each of these images carefully to indicate that the *essence* of each being – diamond, rose, water -- has not been touched, is not beyond recall or rejuvenation. Unfortunately, I think people are often operating with a much more damaged image of our relationship due to original sin – a diamond fractured beyond repair, a rose dying beyond hope, polluted water which can never be cleaned up.

Listen to one of the prayers from the Byzantine liturgy for Christmas!

> Come, let us rejoice in the Lord! Let us proclaim the present mystery by which the partition has been broken and the flaming sword withheld; now shall the Cherubim let us all come to the Tree of life. As for me, I am returning to the bliss of paradise whence I had been driven by original sin.

In the West, Pope St. Leo proclaims the same truth in one of his Christmas sermons:

> In the fullness of time, chosen in the unfathomable depths of God's wisdom, the Son of God took for himself our common humanity in order to reconcile it with its Creator... He took pity on us... so that in him we might be a new creation. Christian, remember your dignity, and now that you share in God's own nature, do not return by sin to your former base condition.... You have been brought into the light of God's kingdom.

"Return to the bliss of paradise." "Reconciliation with the creator." "New creation." "Sharers in God's own nature." "Brought into the light of God's kingdom." Whatever original sin is, it is not more powerful — nowhere near as powerful – as these positive realities.

We have an image of the Redemption something like this. We are drowning. Jesus comes along in a boat and rescues us from the water. But the rest of our life is like being exhausted and soaking wet, hanging over the side of the boat until we reach the shore -- heaven.

It is something much more profound and magnificent than that ! Not only has Jesus pulled us out of the water and into the boat. He has rowed the boat to shore, given us warm clothes, made breakfast for us on the shore, seated us around the cozy fire. The most astounding of all, he sits down with us and explains, as to his intimate friends, the secrets of the kingdom of God. If we believed more in the reality of the Spirit within us, we would experience even now more of the beauty and peace and harmony of the new creation which is both in us and around us.

It was the intensification of this truth that flooded my being that blessed night. I stayed up for two hours, just walking under the stars in the presence of the risen Christ. I knew he was really risen, and that everything against us – original sin, our personal sins, the devil, fear of death, the sin of the world, sickness -- all these had already been conquered by the risen Christ. They would – could – actually be visibly conquered if all the world believed in the risen Christ.

It was a sublime evening. The stars were singing, the waves were gently washing the shore, the wind was blowing – and I was walking in the garden with my God.

In the morning I went to the church of the Loaves and Fishes and celebrated Mass over that exquisite mosaic. I asked pardon for my lack of faith in the Eucharist, my lack of faith in God's providential care for me. He always has taken care of me, and I'm sure he always will. " 'When I broke the seven loaves for the four thousand, how many full hampers of fragments did you collect ?' They answered, 'Seven.' He said to them again, 'Do you still not understand ?' " (Mark 8:20-21)

I prayed too for the people at Madonna House who grow and prepare food for us constantly. They often seem to multiply food miraculously from only five loaves and two fishes.

NAZARETH

On this day I also was planning to visit Nazareth. As I was standing at the bus stop an army truck pulled up and a young Israeli solier asked if I wanted a ride to Tiberias. Of course I did. He was very kind. He had stopped completely unsolicited. He couldn't speak English very well, but said he and his wife were expecting their first child soon and were very excited. (I thought of St. Jospeh and his excitement over his "first born.") I told him I was a Catholic priest, and that I would pray for a safe delivery. He dropped me off at the bus station.

On the bus to Nazareth I read in the paper of Jerusalem's first test-tube baby born in the Hadassah Hospital in Ein Karem. Ein Karem is where the baby in Elizabeth's womb leapt for joy at the presence of Christ in Mary. The process of procreation is becoming more and more separated from human love and the natural processes. We are still adolescents in our human development, manipulating the laws of nature and not supplant her, how to work *with* God's laws and not proudly think we are creating them.

Besides being the town where the Lord spent most of his life, Nazareth had another significance for me: the spirituality of Nazareth is very central in Catherine Doherty's thinking. It is assuming more and more theological importance in my own thinking as well. In very many important writings to the community she says that Madonna House is the spirit of Nazareth, a holy family like that of Jesus, Mary, and Joseph, living ordinary human existence with extraordinary love. You might say that Nazareth is the central mystery of Christ, the "divine milieu," the spiritual atmosphere, in which we are called to live. In Nazareth I would be touching, in still another way, the deep roots of my present way of life.

I said that Nazareth is assuming more importance in my own thinking as well. This may sound like an exorbitant claim, but I really believe the mystery of Nazareth is one of the great keys to the restoration, the re-creation of the whole world. But we do not take his thirty years in Nazareth seriously. Jesus spent most of his life in preparation for his mission.

All the politics, art, economics, culture of the world is diseased because the human person who creates them is diseased. It's like trying to play beautiful music on a broken violin. First the violin must be restored. I believe that if first we lived with the Holy Family in Nazareth for thirty years, learned how to pray, love, purify our hearts – allow Jesus the Master Craftsman to restore the violin – then we could venture forth and play beautiful music. And the music would be new compositions of the Spirit. Nazareth is not simply "getting strength" to infuse the structures of the world with a little sprinkling of the Gospel. Jesus has come to do much, much more than that. He didn't pay much attention to the structures of his day because they were all diseased, beyond repair. Or rather, they are all useless violins, not worth repairing. Jesus has come to build new instruments on which he can play new music. Until our instruments are repaired, we cannot even see what political, artistic, economic music we ought to play. Yes, allowing Jesus to repair us is the great key to the restoration of the world. And it can happen in Nazareth.

I only spent one afternoon in Nazareth. Mostly I just walked around this town where Jesus lived so long. Perhaps some of the people I passed in the streets were his descendants. Possible.

I went, of course, to the main Basilica, where over the entrance it reads, not simply *Verbum Caro Factum Est,* but *Hic – Here,* the Word Became Flesh. Again, I prostrated, in thanksgiving for Mary's fiat. There is an inner shrine (sections of the house of the Holy Family, I think; I'm not sure) which is usually not open or accessible to the public; but you can look through an iron grate.

The grate, at this moment, was open. A priest was arranging flowers on the altar, so I went in and sat down and began to pray. The

I went of course to the main Basilica where over the entrance it reads, not simply Verbum Caro Factum Est, but Hic—-Here the Word Became Flesh... So here I was again, trapped in a very holy place!

priest left, and I remained. I prayed for about fifteen minutes, and then decided to see the rest of the church. But the grate was locked ! Not again ! The priest saw me in here. Why did he lock the grate ?

So here I was again, trapped in a very holy place. O happy fault ! No one hardly ever gets in here. Another gift from God. So I sat down again and kept on praying. I asked for a share in our Lady's profound acceptance of God's will for her, which led to the salvation of the whole human race. What absolute power is unleashed upon the world when we say yes to God with our whole being. After an hour I decided to leave. But how ?

I went to the grate and motioned a priest passing by to come over. I asked him to find someone to unlock the grate. Then I heard a voice from the balcony above, "Father Bob !" It was Sr. Donna ! She came down and we conversed through the grate. "I keep getting locked into these holy places," I said. "Do you think there's some sort of message here ?" We both laughed. In a few minutes a priest came with the keys. He didn't even seem surprised that I was in there. He let me out without saying a word. The whole episode was very mysterious.

I also went to visit the Little Sisters of Jesus in Nazareth. Eddie Doherty, Catherine's husband, had been ordained a priest of the Melkite rite in their chapel by Archbishop Raya in 1969. More roots. Sr. Bernadette was a very gracious host during my brief visit. I spent some time praying in the chapel, mostly thanking God for Fr. Eddie, for his ordination, and for the continuing gift he is to our family. (He was a favorite confessor here. He always gave out three

Alleluias for a penance no matter what you did!) Then I returned to Tabgha.

That night I took my usual walk with the risen Christ along the shore. I thought of one of my favorite stories from the desert fathers. A hundred-year old hermit, every night in the light of the moon, used to take a stroll with his pet lion! It's one of my favorite images of the return to paradise. There he is, all ready to meet Christ. He has been purified; his face is radiant. He's just waiting for Christ to come and take him home.

Early in the morning I celebrated a Mass of the Transfiguration in preparation for climbing Mt. Tabor, which was next on my pilgrimage. After Mass I went swimming in the lake. It was beautiful! The sun was just above the horizon, and there was a brilliant corridor of light coming from the sun to where I was in the water. People who have had a "life after life" experience describe themselves walking down a corridor of light, with a Presence at the far end, drawing them. Jesus was at the end of that corridor of light on the lake that morning. In my imagination I heard him call my name, "Robert! Come!" One day the sound will be real.

As I came out of the water I wondered why so few people who live here believe in Christ. Has God come too close?

TABOR

In a homily once I called the Feast of the Transfiguration the feat of a "good self-image." Here, on this mount, Jesus revealed his divinity as much as human nature could bear. At the same time he revealed our own beauty as "sharers of the divine nature."

One day the Lord revealed to St. Theresa of Avila the beauty of a soul living by the divine life. She said afterwards that, had it not been for the sustaining power of God, she would have "died from too much beauty." To die from too much beauty! This must be what God protects us from in heaven for all eternity.

Even though the bus let me off near Tabor, it was still a long walk to the top, about five miles. A man was sitting by the road and said, "Take a taxi." I said, "No, Jesus walked. I want to walk." He smiled.

It is an extremely winding road up to the top of Tabor. Someone told me how many turns there are, but I forgot. Often the road winds away from the summit, and sometimes even down. As I was walking, this circuitous road became an image of the spiritual life. If we presevere in walking, we are always ascending, even though at times we seem to be walking away from the heights. Our spiritual experience is not one of a continual climbing straight up. There are turns and level runs; but if we keep walking we really are always ascending.

It was a very fatiguing climb, hot and dusty. Taxis were a continual temptation. But I walked along with the Lord, and with Peter and James and John. It must have been exhausting for them as well. Perhaps Peter was thinking: "*Now* where are we going! Do we have to climb to the *top* of this thing!" Bodily penance prepares for grace. The fatigue of the climb was meant to help them withstand the light that was coming. Penance strengthens us to see God and

It was a very fatiguing climb to Tabor, hot and dusty. Taxis were a continual temptation.

not expire from the blaze of light.

On the summit of Tabor, near the church, a group of Jewish boys and girls were having an outing. I wondered if they knew their great ancestors - Moses and Elias – had had an outing here as well. Unfortunately the main church was locked, and wouldn't be open for another three hours. I couldn't wait that long. I sat outside on the stone steps overlooking the panorama below. I waited for the Presence.

Tabor was a very quiet experience for me. No blazing light, no overwhelming vision. I read the Transfiguration story from my New Testament, but I can't say any new insights came to me. It was just "wonderful to be here."

I got up and began walking around. Then I came to the spot where the Lord had been planning to meet me. It wasn't the sight of the Transfiguration, but one of the resurrection appearances. "Then the eleven disciples went to Galilee, to the mountain where Jesus had told them to go."

This mountain traditionally is Tabor. "When they saw him, they worshipped him; but some doubted. Then Jesus said to them, 'All authority in heaven and on earth has been given to me. Therefore go and make disciples of all nations, baptizing them in the name of the Father and of the Son and of the Holy Spirit, and teaching them to obey everything I have commanded you. And surely I will be with you always, to the very end of the ages' " (Matt.28:16-20).

This site was my Presence on Tabor. I thought I had been to all the resurrection sites, but I had forgotten this one. Now I had been to them all. On Tabor, during their first visit with the Lord, the disciples were overcome with Beauty, and wanted to stay on the mountain in contemplation. After the Resurrection, Jesus did not overwhelm them with glory, at least not as before. Surely after his Resurrection he was glorious. But now was the time for mission, for spreading his Good News to the nations. It was not the time to remain for days on the summit.

Christ is beautiful, and at times he wants us to contemplate his beauty; we all need that for our journey. But most of this contemplation is reserved for heaven. Even if one spends a lifetime of prayer in solitude, the deepest call is to mission — to intercession and penance for the world. Someone has said: "May I never be so lost in God that I cannot hear the cries of my brothers and sisters."

Our Tabor experiences cannot remain pure beauty for long. I believe God himself gives us Tabor experiences, like he did the Apostles, but ordinarily they are brief. There is much work to do on the plains. We would simply follow God: be grateful when we experience God as Beauty; draw strength and support from this as he certainly intends us to do. But the total Christ – Christ joined to his Body – is still marred and disfigured. In some real way the total beauty of Christ is not yet a reality. It is for this we pray and work and strive.

There was one final insight on Tabor. I meditated on Jesus appearing to the disciples after his Resurrection. Yes, his life had been hard; he had been rejected by his own; his passion on the Cross was unimaginable. And yet...and yet, he was God, not just another great man. How difficult was the whole task for *God?*

I received a profound sense of Christ's divinity on Tabor. He was *God*. He had really been Lord of everything all the time. Our sins, our blindness, or mindless blocking of his plans, Satan, death itself—nothing could really stop him from saving us. And now this God, this Christ, this God-Man, was now sending me out to preach his Gospel. He would always be at my side.

I walked down the mountain with a new confidence and assurance that I *could* preach his Gospel, and that he *would* be with me. I had been given a greater desire to be his voice and his heart.

On the way down the mountain, my path and that of the group of young people kept criss-crossing. I wondered if they knew I was their real spiritual father.

At Tabgha the next morning I again went swimming in the "Sea of Holy Water," as I began to call it. I concelebrated Mass with my two gracious Franciscan hosts. The psalm verse again was: "I rejoiced when I heard them say, let us go to God's house. And now our feet are standing, within your gates, O Jerusalem." The Gospel was that of the miraculous catch of fish and Peter's confession.

Unlike leaving Jerusalem, I felt a touch of sadness this morning. I had had such an experience of the return to paradise here. In some way I was leaving the garden again!

EPILOGUE

The following critical comment probably wouldn't come from anyone who has profited from this book; it would come from people who pass it by as irrelevant: "My goodness! the world is being over-run by atheistic Communism, people are starving to death in Africa, thousands are being killed in wars. What does making a pilgrimage and writing a book about it have to do with anything!"

Well, the book isn't really about a pilgrimage to Israel. It's about Christ. I went to Israel, of course, but, after all, Gregory of Nyssa is right: we don't have to go to those places. Christ is now risen, and he is everywhere. Jerusalem and the Mount of Olives and Gethsemane and Bethany and Bethlehem and Calvary and the Holy Sepulchre and Nazarath and Tabor and the Mount of the Beatitudes and the charcoal fire on the shore – these mysteries are everywhere now. Christ is all in all, and openness to these ever-present mysteries is the meaning of life, the power to live life. Jerusalem is New York and Bethlehem is Berlin and Nazareth is Paris. Christ is risen, and you can meet him anywhere.

But you must have faith. The greatest, the most tragic wound in the modern world is lack of faith in Christ. It was Christ who brought the pagan world out of darkness, and loss of faith in him which has plunged the world back into darkness. All the isms and philosophies, past and present, which have attempted to lead the human race out of sin and darkness have failed, and they will continue to fail. There is no way out except Christ. As he told us: 'I am the Way."

Well, the book isn't really about a pilgrimage to Israel. It's about Christ.

I believe the key to the restoration and healing of the whole world is the restoration of the human heart. Only Christ, however, can re-create a living person. Whatever helps to re-create the human person in Christ adds to the restoration of the world at the deepest level, the only level where it can and must happen.

We are all pilgrims. Our span of life on the earth is an imperceptible movement of the hand on the atomic clock. The key to making this pilgrimage life-giving and fruitful is openness to the presence of Christ. Unless we are open to the presence of Christ along the road, the atheism and the hunger and the killings will continue until the end of time. We must be open to the presence of Christ and our Lady and the saints as we travel.

If all this sounds "medieval," you are right: it is medieval. Many aspects of the middle ages are eternal truths which we have discarded to our detriment and harm. Would that once again we all had the simple faith of the pilgrims of the middle ages, and walked our paths of life in the company of Christ. For Christ waits for us everywhere now. And if you have faith, if you wait on the Presence, you will experience the fullness of earthly life, and a foretaste of life everlasting.

END

CONTENTS

Introduction.......................... 3

Chapter One:
   Preparation 13

Chapter Two:
   Departure and Arrival................. 30

Chapter Three:
   Jerusalem: Via Dolorosa,
      Mt. of Olives..................... 49

Chapter Four:
   Jerusalem: Cenacle Emmaus,
      Mass at the Holy Sepulchre 76

Chapter Five:
   Bethlehem: Milk Grotto,
      Mar Saba, Cave, Shepherds' Field 96

Chapter Six:
   Jericho, Bethany, Farewell
      to Jerusalem..................... 122

Chapter Seven:
   Galilee: Tabgha, Nazareth,
      Tabor 137

Epilogue 163

www.ingramcontent.com/pod-product-compliance
Lightning Source LLC
Chambersburg PA
CBHW071432160426
43195CB00013B/1876